Handbook of Logic

E. R. EMMET
Assistant Master, Winchester College

1967

LITTLEFIELD, ADAMS & CO.
Totowa, New Jersey

1967 Edition
By LITTLEFIELD, ADAMS & CO.

Published 1966 by Philosophical Library, Inc.,

All rights reserved.

© E. R. EMMET 1960

Printed in the United States of America

Preface

THE object of this book is to help and encourage those who read it to think more clearly. I believe that in our educational system to-day insufficient attention is given to this objective, and that the most effective way to achieve it is by a direct study of the principles of valid reasoning.

There is a danger, however, with the study of logic, even at quite an elementary level, that the student may feel that the subject is one which, like Pure Mathematics or Sanskrit, may provide a good intellectual discipline but has only a remote connection with his everyday thinking. There is also a danger that a work on clear thinking, in attempting to avoid this pitfall, may become chatty and informal and lacking in rigour. I have tried to steer a course between these two extremes, to relax the rigidity of formal logic and to show its limitations, and at the same time to show how much more confidently concepts can be handled and how much more clearly everyday processes of argument can be analysed if the rules and methods of thinking have been systematically and to some extent formally studied.

It has seemed to me important to provide opportunities for practising the applications of the lessons I have tried to teach. For this purpose there is a large number of examples to which hints and solutions are supplied at the end of the book. It has not been easy to pursue a consistent policy about these. When the questions are such as to admit of definite, unique solutions these have been given, and for the harder questions of this kind a method of solution has been indicated. The answers to many questions, however, are, at least to some extent, matters of opinion and I am well aware that the solutions I have suggested,

v

perhaps especially in chapter 9, may not command general agreement. I apologise if in attempting to be brief I have sometimes appeared dogmatic and hope that what I have said may at least provide a basis for discussion.

Inevitably in writing a book like this one is indebted to more authors than one can catalogue or identify. I am also very grateful for advice and encouragement in correspondence and discussion to Mr. C. V. Durell, Professor R. B. Braithwaite, Mr. R. C. Lyness and Mr. J. P. Hudson. To the members of Senior Science Division at Winchester over a period of years I am indebted not only for the constantly stimulating effect of their questions and comments on the subject matter of these pages but also for many of the passages offered for analysis and criticism and the testing of many of the problems. My thanks also to Mrs. J. H. Preston for her skill and patience in deciphering and typing.

Acknowledgments

We are indebted to the following for permission to quote copyright material:

Messrs. Basil Blackwell & Mott Ltd. for an extract from *The Foundation of Arithmetic* by C. Frege, trans. by J. L. Austin; The Controller of Her Majesty's Stationary Office for the use of the Table of Population Figures taken from the *Monthly Digest of Statistics* for April 1958; The Editor of the *Daily Express* for an extract from the August 25th, 1955 issue; Mr. D. A. Ferguson and the Editor of *The Times* for material from the August 18th, 1958 issue; Messrs. Victor Gollancz Ltd. and Random House Inc. New York for an extract from *Guide to Philosophy* by C. E. M. Joad; Mr. R. D. Goodall and the Editor of *The Times* for material from the November 23rd, 1954 issue; Mr. H. D. P. Lee and Messrs. Penguin Books Ltd. for extracts from *Plato's Republic*; Sir Hugh Linstead, M.P., and the Editor of *The Times* for material from the August 16th, 1958 issue; The Oxford University Press for extracts from *A Study of History* by A. J. Toynbee; Mr. E. C. Philips for material from the October 21st, 1955 issue of the *Daily Express*; Mr. Richard Pilkington, M.P. for material from the February 10th, 1957 issue of the *Sunday Times*; Dr. A. S. Thomas and the Editor of *The Times* for material from the August 30th, 1957 issue; and Messrs. J. Whitaker & Sons Ltd. for the use of figures taken from *Whitaker's Almanac*.

Contents

I

Introduction

EVERYBODY knows in a general sort of way what it is to think; and anyone who is reading this and understanding it is 'thinking' just as the author writing it was 'thinking', though no one could claim that his thought was very profound. But most people take the operation of thinking for granted and are not in the habit of analysing it closely and examining the rules and principles according to which it is carried on. It will be the object of this book to do these things.

One of the major purposes of education is to teach people to think clearly. But it is curious that there is not often much attempt to do this by any direct method. The young are taught disciplines in which to a varying extent there is need for clear thinking, and it is hoped (sometimes without very much justification) that they will then be able to think clearly about other things. Classics and Mathematics are examples of such disciplines. In order to be successful as a Classic or a Mathematician—for example in order to get a University Scholarship—it is undoubtedly necessary to be able to think clearly and effectively along particular lines, but it does not necessarily follow that the student who has acquired this ability will be able to apply it to other fields of thought.

Perhaps we shall think more effectively if we think about our thinking more.

Much of our thinking is *undirected*, as when, sitting in an armchair after a pleasant dinner, we remember the delights of our week by the sea or the glory of that run we made in the village cricket match. It might perhaps be objected that such reflections or memories should not be dignified by the title of 'thinking', but it would seem most nearly in accordance with modern practice to do so: if asked by a friend what we were thinking about we would be unlikely to say that we were not thinking but remembering. Clearly the more important kind of thinking is that which is *directed*, as when we are trying to put an English sentence into Latin, puzzling over a mathematical problem, planning what we are going to do tomorrow, or reading alertly and critically an article in a newspaper. In each case the thinking is directed towards a specific purpose.

The distinction might also be made by saying that the first kind of thinking is *passive*; we let thoughts come, in a sense, unbidden into our minds. And the second kind is *active*; we have the feeling that we are marshalling, controlling, directing our mental processes.

As so often with distinctions of this kind it would not be hard to find border-line cases, examples of thinking which one would be uncertain whether to classify as directed or undirected, active or passive. But the broad distinction remains a useful one. It is with thinking of the directed, active kind that we shall be almost exclusively concerned in this book.

Both these kinds of thinking may be verbal or non-verbal, with words or without them. When I am remembering the happiest day of my holidays I am almost certainly doing it in a series of recaptured sensations, seeing 'with my mind's eye' that view of the mountains, feeling the invigorating salt water on my limbs, smelling 'with my mind's nose' the heather and the thyme. The present writer finds that the visual memory is the easiest to use and provides the clearest and most satisfactory sensations—that his 'mind's eye' in other words, is usually more efficient than his 'mind's nose' or his 'mind's ears'—but the experience of other people about this may be quite different.

Again when I am making a plan for the future—how I shall spend tomorrow, how I shall pipe the water to my mountain cottage, what my next move shall be in a game of chess—my thinking may take place almost entirely in pictures, though it may also be accompanied by a running mental commentary (. . . 'if I play golf with Smith it won't be much of a game for him' . . . 'Is my pipe long enough if I start from there?' . . . 'If I move my bishop there he takes me with his knight, I take with my pawn. . . .') We may be thinking here partly with, partly without, words but there is no reason at all in every one of these three cases why the thinking should not all take place without words.

Clearly, however, if one is putting an English sentence into Latin any thinking that is to be of any use for that purpose must be in words—either English or Latin; and if one is reading critically an article in a newspaper most, but not I think necessarily *all*, of one's thinking about it will be in words.

But whatever the extent to which we can do our thinking without words—and there is certainly considerable variation from person to person about this—there is no doubt that as soon as we start to try to communicate our thoughts to other people words are almost essential. When, by being asked to write an essay about it, the schoolboy is compelled to put into words his recollections of the happiest day of the holidays he is faced with a double difficulty. First he has to describe in words what probably exists in his mind as a series of pictures—the family walking up Snowdon, the picnic lunch on the way (both of these are pictures in which the schoolboy sees himself included), the view from the top (this will be a picture simply of what he saw), the bathe in the sea in the evening, and the special dinner which crowned this special day. He has to select the words and the sentences which will effectively tell his form-master what in fact he did that day: he is being tested (and this is clearly the form-master's intention) in his ability to describe his experience accurately, grammatically and attractively.

The second difficulty is to describe not merely what happened in the course of the day but what there was about it which made it the *happiest*. This is the difficulty of communicating the flavour or the value of the experiences and it might not be what the form-master intended: it is certainly a very much harder thing to do. However well or badly he does it the schoolboy is being given practice in putting his mental images—of sight, or sound, or taste, or feeling—into words so that he can communicate his experience to others.

The communication of the pleasures of an experience is particularly difficult, but if I am asked to put into words my deliberations about what I shall do tomorrow, it ought not to be hard to convey effectively to my hearer the various plans I have in mind and the arguments for and against each of them. And it is very likely that the expression of my thoughts in words may make it easier for me to make up my mind what to do, partly because I may have expressed them more clearly in words than in pictures, and partly because by putting them into words I compel myself, as it were, to think out thoroughly the various pros and cons, whereas if they remained non-verbal my thoughts might merely be vague and half-formed. Whether we think better with or without words depends partly on the nature of the subject: it also depends on how good we are at using words. Most of us have probably had the experience of being asked what we are thinking and replying, 'Well, it's rather hard to put it into words.' This may be because we feel that words are inadequate to express the elevated or profound thought that is ours at the moment—that if we put it into words it will appear trite or feeble. Or it may be because we feel with a proper humility that we are not sufficiently skilled at wielding these delicate instruments. It may be, in other words, because we feel that there are not any tools in existence that will do the job, or it may be because we feel that although the tools are there we do not know how to use them properly.

But it is clearly important to learn, and many of us find that our thinking about a variety of subjects becomes clearer if we sit down, pen in hand, and compel our thoughts to take verbal shape. And even if this is not so there can be no doubt that our thinking in general is more likely to be useful if we can communicate the results to others, and we can usually only do this by putting them into words.

NON-VERBAL COMMUNICATION

But although words are usually necessary for communication they are not always. It is worth examining briefly the sort of communication that takes place without words.

If you were in a foreign country of whose language you were quite ignorant you would not have much difficulty in indicating the fact that you were hungry or thirsty. You would probably do this by pointing and by miming the actions of eating and drinking. When people talk to each other they almost always—to some extent unconsciously—supplement the words they are saying by facial expressions or by gestures. Some people, for example the French and Italians, do this to a considerable extent and a Frenchman may 'say' as much with his hands, his arms, his shoulders, his eyebrows as he does with his words. Sometimes such gestures may take the place of words: more often they supplement them.

The world around us is full of examples of non-verbal communication—traffic-lights at a cross-roads, S-bend signs, an umpire at cricket signalling a 'wide'. And anyone who has had much experience of using a map will appreciate the amount of detailed information which can be imparted by the non-verbal symbols there employed. It should be noticed, however, that deaf and dumb language, semaphore or Morse code are not instances of non-verbal communication; they are simply examples of the letters and words being expressed and communicated in ways other than speaking or writing.

In all these examples of non-verbal communication the thought expressed is a simple one. Obviously the more complex the thought the harder it is to communicate it without words and very often, too, the harder it is to think it without words.

In the next chapter we shall attempt to examine very much more closely these essential implements of thought.

2

Words

WE have seen that for thoughts to be communicated they must usually be put into words, and that words almost always help us to think more clearly and effectively.

Words are obviously of very great importance to mankind, but they must be kept in their place; they must be always the servants of our thinking and not its masters. We must remember that it is we, men and women, who constructed the words in the first place and who collectively decide, under the guidance to some extent of schoolmasters, linguists and so forth, how they shall be used. We must beware always of thinking that because a word exists the 'thing' for which that word is supposed to stand necessarily exists too.

As John Stuart Mill said:

> The tendency has always been strong to believe that whatever receives a name must be an entity or being, having an independent existence of its own: and if no real entity answering to the name could be found, men did not for that reason suppose that none existed, but imagined that it was something peculiarly abstruse and mysterious, too high to be an object of sense.

To take a simple case, it is not necessarily true that because the words 'unicorn', 'centaur' exist there are in nature animals for which the words stand. This seems obvious to us now, but it was not always so.

Or again, to take a more complex example, though it may be convenient and intelligible to talk of a man having a strong Will

B

or a good Memory, or a powerful Reason, it is generally agreed by psychologists today that this division of the personality into departments such as 'Will', 'Memory', 'Reason' is erroneous and misleading and that these words cannot rightly be thought of as standing for real entities.

Primitive men used to think of words as instruments for the control of objects and they often attributed supernatural power to them. As Ogden and Richards tell us in *The Meaning of Meaning:*

> Every ancient Egyptian had two names—one for the world, and another by which he was known to the supernatural powers. The Abyssinian Christian's second name, given at baptism, is never to be divulged. The guardian deity of Rome had an incommunicable name, and in parts of ancient Greece the holy names of the gods, to ensure against profanation, were engraved on lead tablets and sunk in the sea.

These are examples of what we should regard as superstitious importance being attached to the names given to people; they are cases therefore where there is a danger of words assuming a mastery that should not be theirs. In modern times the danger is more subtle—the danger that abstract nouns like Communism or Democracy may be venerated or abused for themselves without reference to the ideas for which they are supposed to stand, and may unduly influence man's thinking. We must be aware the whole time of the danger of allowing our methods of thinking to be dictated too much (it is bound to happen to some extent) by the language we have inherited and the ways in which it has been used in the past.

Words, therefore, must, in one way, not be regarded as too important: they are merely tools. But just because they are tools they are in another sense very important indeed.

A carpenter will be unable to do his work efficiently unless he has at his disposal tools which are exactly the right ones for the job he has in hand. The important thing is that they should be appropriate—accurate, well-sharpened, precise, or heavy and blunt according to what is required. And the carpenter must know how to use them.

Although these tools are of the greatest importance to him, if he is a good carpenter they are his servants. In the short run it may be true that the work he can do will be dictated to him by the nature and variety of the tools he has at his disposal and the condition they are in. But in the long run he will not allow his work to be impeded in this way: he will get new and better tools, devising original ones if necessary, and he will see to it that those he has are kept in first-rate condition for the jobs for which he is going to use them.

The analogy between a carpenter and his tools and a thinker and his words is a useful one. We must have words which we know how to use and which aptly express the thoughts we have in mind. But in what sense can words be described, even metaphorically, as accurate and well-sharpened?

Suppose that I say or write: 'Tables are usually made of wood.' There would be little doubt that this sentence would successfully convey the meaning I have in mind. We all know pretty well what we mean by 'table': we all know more exactly what we mean by 'wood': and though 'usually' is a rather vague word there would probably be agreement if I said I intended 'at least more often than not'. If you were setting out to pick holes in what I say you might question the truth of this statement by asserting that in some primitive countries rocks are used as tables and that if all those were to be included the number made of wood would be only a minority. You might say 'what *exactly* do you mean by table? Is it defined by its size, its shape, the number of its legs or the purpose for which it is used?'

But although it would be possible to ask troublesome questions about this statement, they would for the most part be questions asked by someone who was *trying* to be troublesome. On the whole the words used are sufficiently 'accurate' and 'well-sharpened' to do the job for which I am using them: that is they communicate to my listeners or readers the thought which I have in my mind.

Suppose now that I say, 'Democracy is a good thing.' The meaning that is communicated and the reaction that results will of course depend very much on the context and occasion. A word like 'democracy' today is so charged with emotional associations that many people would find it difficult to write down a clear, coherent account of what they suppose is meant by anyone who uses the word. And if one did get, say, a dozen different people to write down what they would mean their accounts would be likely to differ considerably. One would also get widely different accounts about what was meant by 'being a good thing' in this context.

The words 'Democracy' and 'good' in this sentence are not 'accurate' or 'well-sharpened'. I might say that they do not enable me to perform the task of communicating my thoughts clearly. But it must be admitted that the thought that inspired such a sentence is likely to have been vague, hazy and altogether slovenly; in which case it might perhaps be more accurate to say that these words do not enable me, or at any rate do not help me, to *think* accurately and clearly. If asked what exactly I meant by the sentence I should have to do some hard thinking, and I should have to find and to use words which were capable of conveying a more precise meaning.

If a word, then, is to be described as accurate it must be the sort of word to which different people will attach the same meaning and that meaning must be a reasonably clear-cut and precise one. That is true of the words 'table' and 'wood', but it is not true of the words 'democracy' and 'good'.

In order to get a clearer idea of the difficulties involved here—

how it is that some words can be described as accurate while others cannot—it will be well to examine more closely how we decide or discover what a word is going to be used to mean.

OSTENSIVE DEFINITION

An example of the simplest use of a word or symbol is when we point to a succession of similar animals and say 'cat', 'cat', 'cat'....

This is a way of announcing that we intend to use the word or symbol 'cat' to refer to animals of this type. It would not be sufficient to point to one animal for 'cat' might then be its name or might stand for any four-legged animal. The word in a sense 'stands for' the animal but it is important to notice that the word is nothing unless someone uses it, i.e. writes it or says it. *We* use the word to refer to the object. It might be said loosely that the word 'cat' *means* an animal of this type but strictly speaking it is *we* who mean. It will be an aid to clear thinking about this if, instead of asking ourselves what various words mean, we ask what the people who use them mean. And if a word is to be used for effective communication there must be general agreement that different people will mean the same thing.

To explain how a word is going to be used and what we are going to make it stand for is to *define* it, and if this explanation takes place by pointing or its equivalent the process is called *ostensive definition*. We explain how we intend to use the word 'cat' by pointing to or displaying a number of those animals.

There are clearly very many words that can be defined ostensively in this way ... nouns like 'chair', 'animal', 'house', 'waistcoat'; adjectives like 'red', 'hard', 'square'; verbs like 'to walk', 'to dance', 'to swallow', 'to hit'; prepositions like 'under', 'in', 'from', 'through'. In some cases if one wants to define the word very precisely—if for example a biologist is drawing a distinction between animal and plant life—the production of a sufficient num-

ber of examples to make it clear ostensively where the line is to be
drawn might be difficult and tedious and it would be convenient
to supplement the ostensive definition with a verbal one.

But in the beginnings of language definition must clearly be
ostensive, just as a Frenchman and a German who have no language in common can only communicate with each other by first
making signs and then by teaching each other their language by
ostensive definition.

VERBAL DEFINITION

The other method we have of explaining what we mean by a
word, or defining it, is to do so in terms of other words—*verbal
definition*. If I am trying to explain to someone what a cat is and
there is not one available to which I can point I might say: 'It's a
four-legged animal with fur, usually about two feet long. . . .'

The answer might be, from A, 'Oh, yes. I know what you
mean: I've seen lots of those about, but I didn't know they were
called cats.'

Or from B, 'I don't think I've ever seen any of those, but I can
imagine what it's like. I suppose it's about the size of a small dog.
And I know what fur is, my aunt's got a fur coat.'

From C, 'I don't understand what you're talking about.
What's an animal? How can anything have *four* legs? What's
fur?'

A has already been shown the object that is being defined but
he hasn't had it linked for him to the word which is going to be
used to stand for it. The verbal definition works because it succeeds in linking the word 'cat' with the object, cat, which has
been experienced.

B, however, has no experience of cats but he has seen four-
legged animals and fur and he is capable of linking these ideas
together. The verbal definition works, at least to some extent,
because it succeeds in linking the word 'cat' with separate experi-

ences of the different characteristics of the object, cat, which are then brought together in the mind.

But it is almost certain that the idea of cat for B will be much less clear than for A. B might now be able to recognize a cat as such, but if he were asked to draw a picture of one it would probably not be very convincing.

But for C the verbal definition is a complete failure. He has not experienced any of the things referred to, his mind has got nothing to work on. I might try again to explain what an animal is and what fur is and I should clearly have to search for ideas that he has experienced. If I can find none my task is hopeless.

Inevitably, verbal definition is circular and by itself it is useless: we define cat as an animal with fur, and we define fur as what a cat has. The definition, the explanation, can only succeed in communicating our meaning if it is composed of words whose meanings have already been understood: and in the last resort, or rather in the first resort, these meanings must have been made clear by ostensive definition.

It is impossible, for example, to explain what red looks like to someone who has been blind from birth, for there is nothing in his experience to which any of the words can be made to refer.

In practice when we are defining words we generally use both kinds of definition: we may start with a verbal definition but if we are sensible we use ostensive definition whenever possible to supplement and clarify our meaning.

DENOTATION AND CONNOTATION

It is worth drawing attention here to a distinction made by logicians which is very similar to that between ostensive and verbal definition. We have seen that if we are asked what is meant by a 'rose' there are two methods of answering. The first method is to take the enquirer out into the garden, if it is the right time of year, and point to a variety of roses: in other words to define 'rose' ostensively. Ideally, in order to complete this ostensive definition we should be able to point to all the roses there are. The whole class of 'roses' is said to be what the word 'rose' 'denotes', or is the '*denotation*' of 'rose'.

Our other method of answering would be to explain what it is to be a 'rose', that is to explain the characteristics and attributes of the flower. In order to do this properly we should have to be expert botanists and to know the technical vocabulary. To do this would be to define verbally what it is to be a rose; the qualities and attributes of a rose are called the '*connotation*' of 'rose'.

The '*denotation*' of a class is thus simply all members of the class: the '*connotation*' of a class is a description of the qualifications for membership of the class. The denotation of 'car-owner' is all those people who own cars, the connotation is simply the characteristic of owning a car.

ACCURACY OF DEFINITION

It is not hard to see how the meaning of words which are capable of ostensive definition is built up. Sometimes and for some purposes it is convenient to make the meaning very precise, at other times it may not very much matter how precise it is. For example in England there is no clear-cut dividing line in ordinary conversation between a town and a village. Usually it does not matter and an argument between two people to decide which it is would generally speaking be a foolish one. But for certain purposes—for example those of local government—it may be desirable to construct a dividing line, to say that if the population is above 3,000 it shall rank as a town, below that as a village. To insist, because of this, that for purposes of ordinary conversation we should first discover the exact population of a place before referring to it as a town or village would be pedantic and silly.

We want our words to be suitable for the purpose for which we are using them: if our purpose is accurate, precise thought we must have accurate, precise words, but it is important to remember that we do not always want our thoughts to be accurate and precise and it is not, therefore, always necessary to have the denotation or connotation of our term accurately defined. In most of our ordinary conversations we are using words the whole time of which the denotation and connotation are vague. And for most of our ordinary conversations it does not matter at all that that is so. We have seen already that we should find it difficult to agree upon a precise connotation for 'table', but as for most purposes we use the word for particular tables . . . ('Put the fish on that table, dear, not on the chair') our thinking and our communication are not in the least hindered by that fact. But it is important to realize that if we start enquiring whether a slab of wood with four legs attached to it, which people mostly use for sitting on, is or is not a table we are not propounding a deep metaphysical question but merely discussing how we shall use a word. And this particular word is one which we are on the whole perfectly happy to leave with a vague connotation. Accuracy and precision are not here necessary for the purposes for which we want the word. We do not need a surgeon's delicate instruments to extract a thorn from our fingers, nor do we need scales which register milligrammes to discover whether we have put on weight in the last ten years.

The words we have considered so far have for the most part been capable of ostensive definition—they stand for simple things like roses or waistcoats, for simple activities like dancing or eating, or for simple qualities like red or square. We can be reasonably certain that for the most part people mean approximately the same thing when they use these words. If they don't, if what I call a waistcoat you call a pullover our disagreements will very soon and very easily be brought to light and will probably be adjusted; perhaps after consulting a third person one of us will agree that his use of the word was not in accordance with common practice and will consent to change it. There will often be border-line disagreements—what is the difference between capering and dancing?—but because the definition is in the first place ostensive these disagreements will usually easily be resolved if it happens to be important for any particular purpose that they should be. The essential thing is to be able to realize whether the disagreement is one about how a certain word is to be used or whether it is a real argument about real things.

This sort of difficulty is much more likely to arise with words that cannot be defined ostensively but it may be worth illustrating the point with a simple example.

Suppose that on my return from the beach I am asked whether there were many people bathing this morning. I reply: 'Yes, a good many.' X, who was with me, says, 'Oh, no, there weren' very many.' We then have a discussion as to whether or not there were many people bathing. It is possible that there might be a serious disagreement about the actual number. I might have seen about 150 whereas X, who is an unobservant type, might only have noticed about a dozen. But it is more likely that we are in rough agreement about the number but disagree about whether to call it 'many'.

I hadn't been down there for a week and there were certainly many more than when last I went, but X who was there yesterday found there were fewer there today. In a sense it might be argued that we are using the word many to mean the same thing, namely, 'as many as or more than we expected' but that it is our expectations which differ. And though we can compare notes about our expectations and about the way in which we use 'many', once we have realized what the discussion is about it is virtually over. It is interesting to notice that we use 'many' according to the context to mean any number from 2 upwards. ('Has X got many wives?') In some ways this flexibility or adaptability may be useful, though there is a danger that it may make a conversation so vague as to be nearly meaningless, and in any talking or writing about mathematical or scientific matters that lays claim to accuracy the word 'many' is almost useless.

ABSTRACT WORDS

Words which cannot be defined ostensively, words such as 'justice', 'value', 'purpose', 'imagining', 'thinking', 'good', 'beautiful', for which there is no concrete thing, or activity or quality to which we can point by way of definition are called *abstract words*.

It is much more difficult in using them to be certain that we mean the same thing and it is therefore much more likely that arguments in which such words occur will be stultified because words are being used to mean different things by different people.

If someone interrupts an argument of this kind by saying: 'It all depends what you mean by . . .' he is often regarded as being pedantic and tiresome, but in fact it is an essential point about which agreement must be reached before any useful discussion can start.

Almost inevitably the process by which we become acquainted with the meanings that are to be attached to abstract words is a gradual one. By reading about 'justice' in several different contexts we come to have a vague idea of what the word is being used to mean. And as we grow older we accumulate more and more references and cross-references to it until we have a whole association of ideas linked with that word.

It is clearly very difficult to discover how closely the complex of ideas aroused in my mind by the word 'justice' resembles that aroused in yours. It is doubly difficult because in the first place I should not find it easy to express those ideas in words—that is, my conception of what I mean by 'justice' is itself vague—and in the second place if I did succeed in putting those ideas into words many of them would inevitably be of the kind which are not capable of ostensive definition, which are therefore themselves linked with a further complex of ideas. The double difficulty therefore repeats itself.

It may not matter that the meaning which a word like 'justice' has is inevitably vague and shifting: what is important again is that we should recognize that this is so and that we should be able to distinguish between an argument in which we really are discussing whether a particular act is just (having clearly defined for our local limited purpose what it is to be just), and one in which we are debating perhaps unconsciously how we are to use the word 'just'.

Suppose, for example, that a schoolmaster is asked whether it was just that Jones Major should have been punished for eating sweets in the class-room while in the same period Smith Minimus was let off with a warning. The schoolmaster might point out that Jones had been warned before, that he had been eating persistently, provocatively and noisily: Smith on the other hand was very minimus, it was his first day at school and it was only a small sweet.

Having had the circumstances explained to him the interrogator might then agree—'Yes—it was just.' But if he did not agree, if they were both in possession of the same set of facts and one thought the action was just and the other did not, then it must be that they are using the word 'just' in different senses, or that they are applying different criteria in deciding what it is to be just. Any further argument about the justice of the action that failed to recognize that it was the meaning of the word that was under discussion would be a futile one. The disputants might of course agree about a verbal definition of 'just': they might both say that by being 'just' they mean 'giving everyone his due' but obviously this merely shifts the question to what is meant by 'due'. If two people with exactly the same information about an event disagree as to whether a certain word should properly be used to describe it then either they are expressing the fact that their attitudes towards the event are different, that one, perhaps, approves and the other disapproves, or it is the use of the word about which they are disagreeing.

There might of course in the example given be further argument as to whether it was *desirable* that Smith should remain unpunished: it might be maintained that to punish him now will have the effect of saving a lot of trouble and sweets in the future, and any discussion about this—the possible effects of a certain action—would be a real discussion and not a verbal one.

It is in abstract thinking that the danger arises most often of allowing words, as it were, 'to take charge'. There is the tendency, to which we have referred earlier, to suppose that there are neat parcels of things in the world of reality corresponding to abstract nouns such as Justice, Faith, Perfection. There is also the tendency in some cases to suppose that words have a single, real, proper meaning if only we could discover what it is. 'Yes,' it might be said, 'I see how you are using the word, but what does it *really* mean?' 'What is the *real* meaning of just or good?'

To think in this way is to be like the person who, when a new planet was discovered and given the name Uranus, asked how the astronomer could be sure that it *really was* Uranus.

The corrective for this tendency—and nearly everybody makes this sort of mistake sometimes—is to remind ourselves the whole time that *we* make the words; the meanings we attach to them are built up, sometimes gradually, by the general agreement of mankind and these meanings are in many cases various and are subject to alteration if people on the whole decide to use them differently.

An example of a word which now conveys a meaning which has significantly changed is 'precarious'. This word is derived from the Latin: *precari* = to pray, and was orginally used to mean 'obtained by entreaty' or 'held at someone else's pleasure'. People use it now almost exclusively to mean 'uncertain', 'liable to be upset' as in 'precariously poised', 'a precarious livelihood'.

It is very easy to see how this change of use has come about. The tenure of anything that is obtained by entreaty or is held at someone's else's pleasure will quite likely, but not necessarily, be uncertain or 'precarious' (in the modern sense of the word). A tenure or position therefore comes to be described as 'precarious' just *because* it is uncertain, without any reference to whether or not it has been obtained by entreaty: and the fact that this was its original meaning may then very quickly be forgotten.

There is a tendency to say of a word like this that the original meaning is its *real* meaning or what it ought to mean and that people who use it to mean merely 'uncertain' are just making a mistake. It is true of course that the new use of the word must have arisen from ignorance in the past and there may have been misunderstandings and failures of communication owing to the fact that different people were using it to mean different things. But now that the change has taken place, however much we may regret it, there is nothing that we can do about it. By using the word in its new sense people successfully convey their meaning, and if as a defiant gesture directed against the processes of change we use the word in its old sense we shall simply fail to make our meaning clear.

It is of course the classical scholar who, because he instinctively notes the derivation of the word, is most likely to regret and resist the change in meaning. And it is worth noticing that it is almost impossible now for there to be any change in the meanings attached to ancient Greek and Latin words: this is simply because they are dead languages and are hardly used at all today for purposes of communication either in speech or in writing. The meanings are firmly under the control of schoolmasters and university dons and are fixed in a way in which the meanings of the words of a living, growing language can never be.

A living language is changed by the adaptation of old words to new uses: it is also added to by the construction of new words. This happens most often in science, especially a science that is exploring new ground. The development of electricity, for example, was accompanied by a whole crop of new words—ohms, ampères, electrons, volts, etc. Such new words may refer to entities which had not previously been known to exist, they may reflect a new way of classifying or looking at reality, or they may be short ways of expressing what could easily be said at greater length with old words.

'Psycho-kinesis' for example is a word that has recently been coined to describe the movement of matter outside a man's body by the exercise of his mind, without using physical means. There was no need for this word earlier because it is only recently that the possibility of such a thing happening has been seriously investigated. But now, for those who are interested, the use of the word saves time and trouble.

Such new words must obviously be carefully defined and if they are going to be employed only in technical contexts it is likely that they will be carefully used, and that there will not be very much danger of the meaning attached to them shifting or changing. Sometimes a new word may be coined for one of the many meanings attaching to a word that is already in existence, for in the pursuit of an accurate train of thought it will be a hindrance both to thinking and communication if the word which normally conveys the meaning one wants to express is also used to convey other meanings, especially if they differ only subtly and slightly from the one that is wanted. This is most likely to happen in subjects such as Psychology, Economics or Philosophy in which the ideas being studied are matters of everyday conversation. For example Sir Dennis Robertson, the eminent economist, uses the word 'Ecfare' to describe the particular aspect of welfare which is economic.

There are many examples in English of the same word being used to mean a variety of things. 'Pound' can be of weight or of money (meanings that are quite different now, though they are connected historically), or an enclosure for cattle, or it can be used as a verb, 'to thump or pummel', or 'to make one's way heavily', meanings which have no very close connection with its use as a noun. It is much less likely to matter if the meanings differ widely for it is usually clear from the context which one is intended and an ambiguity that is obvious is less likely to impede clear thinking and communication than one that is subtle and concealed. If a schoolmaster, for example, has told his mathematical set to bring up log tables and a boy comes staggering into the class-room with a wooden piece of furniture, the incident would probably be regarded as a failure of discipline rather than of communication.

It is natural and right that the creation of new words should be taking place the whole time in a living language. Those that satisfy a popular need will be absorbed into the language and it will soon be forgotten how new they are; others will remain technical words to be used only by scientists; and others will perhaps be used only by the person who invented them and after one appearance in some scientific or philosophical journal will be heard and seen no more.

It is often said that a language is debased when old words change their meanings and new, hybrid words are invented. It is certainly a matter for regret when through carelessness or ignorance or slipshod thinking words are used in such a way that they no longer convey the precise, accurate meaning for which they were originally designed. We can make up our minds to help to resist such debasement by thinking clearly and using words carefully. But we must remember that in a progressive dynamic society in which ideas are changing and in which men are developing new ways of looking at things, it is inevitable and proper that the tools of thinking should be undergoing development, too.

EMOTIONAL ASSOCIATIONS OF WORDS

We have seen that the complex associations of ideas evoked by certain words are not easy to communicate and are likely to differ from person to person.

When language is being used partly or entirely to evoke emotion, as it is often in poetry and in some kinds of prose, this complex of associations is of great importance. Such writing will clearly depend for its effectiveness on the similarity of the associations for different people, or the extent to which the word, the phrase, the sentence, or just the sound, evokes in the reader or the listener emotions similar to those with which it was associated by the writer.

Such associations are continually changing with the passage of time. If a writer today were to use the phrase 'verdant pastures' he would be likely to be accused of being trite or hackneyed, whereas at some time, for some people, that phrase would no doubt have had the most pleasant associations of peace and comfort and beauty. It is very easy to say what 'verdant pastures' *mean*: I could explain it to you ostensively as I write by pointing out of the window, but as an instrument in the evoking of emotion, in the conjuring up of a picture of beauty it is probably for most people no longer efficacious.

The importance of the emotional associations of words for our present purposes lies in the fact that they are likely to be serious hindrances to straight, clear thinking. This is especially true in argument, or when the thinking is expressed in a chain of reasoning which is designed to persuade. It is perhaps almost inevitable that this should happen to some extent: the essential thing is that we should be able to recognize it and allow for it.

If there is a discussion, for example, about the desirability of

c

employing black men in a certain industry the use of the word 'niggers' would not assist a calm, unemotional approach. For most people that word carries a derogatory flavour: it does not merely convey the meaning 'black men' but it also expresses the attitude of the speaker: 'black men of whom I disapprove and I take it for granted that you do too!' It is true that in conversation the same effect could be achieved to some extent by the tone of voice in which the words 'black men' were uttered, but the use of 'nigger' makes it more emphatic still.

There are of course many words or phrases which may be used in such a way as not merely to state a fact but also to express an attitude, and such words and phrases have a useful purpose to fulfil. But when they are being used in what purports to be a rational discussion we must be careful to ensure that they are not used in such a way as to prejudge the issue or beg the question.

It would obviously be foolish to discuss whether it was a good thing to be pig-headed: for 'pig-headed' is normally used to describe someone who in the opinion of the speaker is excessively or unreasonably disinclined to change his mind, and an excess of anything must by definition be a bad thing. If Smith and Jones are discussing Robinson, and Smith says that he has the spirit of eternal youth while Jones says that he is suffering from arrested development they are agreeing about the fact that Robinson is young for his years but their attitudes towards the fact are different. It may be interesting for them to continue to produce phrases of approval and disapproval but they must not delude themselves into thinking that they are having a rational argument.

The use of such emotionally coloured words or phrases in argument may often be unconscious, but they may also be used with dishonest intent. The person who applies the word 'blackmail' to any threat which he dislikes, or 'sabotage' to any action which obstructs the execution of his purposes, is not merely expressing and inviting disapproval, but is also, probably deliberately, misrepresenting facts. 'Blackmail' is still mainly used in its original sense of the threat of revealing some discreditable secret, in other words it is what most people would regard as a particularly base kind of threat; and 'sabotage' is still mainly used to mean the malicious, deliberate destruction of plant, factories, etc. It is possible, of course, that people may use these words so often to make actions which they dislike sound worse than they are that their original meanings may become lost. If this happens it will be interesting to see how long they retain their evil associations and how long, therefore, they are effective for the purpose for which they are used.

This use of words to express an attitude instead of, or perhaps as well as, stating a fact is called the '*emotive*' use of words. Examples abound in ordinary conversation and writing, and they may, of course, be perfectly harmless and legitimate. They are frequently found in the utterances of politicians who are taking part in a controversy, and it is perhaps here, where emotions and loyalties are so easily aroused, that they are most likely to obscure clear thinking. It is here, therefore, that it is particularly important to be on the lookout for them, and to be prepared to analyse them.

SUMMARY

In order to think and communicate clearly we must study words carefully. We must beware of thinking that words have 'real' meanings which are in some mysterious way attached to them. We must think what we use them to mean and we must examine the ways in which they are used by other people.

We must be sure that we are not allowing our thoughts to be blurred and slipshod because we are using words which are defined vaguely when precision is necessary and possible, or using words in a question-begging and emotionally coloured way. It is inevitable and right that we should have our attitudes of approval or disapproval, but we must recognise them for what they are and not confuse them with rational thinking, though they may be part, and a very necessary and important part, of the data in a logical argument.

Our choice of words and the way in which we use them should be related the whole time to the purpose we have in view. If we are using words for communication this purpose may be to inform, to describe, to request, to persuade, to command, to question, to explain, to prove, or some combination of these.

Which words we use and how we use them will obviously depend not only on which of these things we are trying to do, but also on what we know of the intelligence and background of our audience.

Examples on Chapter 2

1. Explain the mistake in saying: 'They're called pigs because they are such dirty animals.'

2. In his book *Among Congo Cannibals* J. H. Weeks writes*: 'I remember on one occasion wanting the word for Table. There were five or six boys standing round, and, tapping the table with my forefinger, I asked, "What is this?" One boy said it was a *dodela*, another that it was an *etanda*, a third stated that it was *bokali*, a fourth it was *elamba*, and the fifth said it was *meẓa*. These various words we wrote in our note-book, and congratulated ourselves that we were working among a people who possessed so rich a language that they had five words for one article.'

   (i) Would you come to the same conclusion? If not, what?

   (ii) Would you think it an advantage for a language to have five words for one article?

* Quoted in *The Meaning of Meaning*, Ogden and Richards.

3. Comment on:

'I do believe, though I have found them not, that there may be
Words which are things.'

(Byron, *Childe Harold*)

4. If asked to explain in writing the meaning of a word it is important to be aware of the state of knowledge of the person to whom one is
supposed to be explaining. In practice it is usually a matter of convincing an examiner that you know how the word is ordinarily used.
There are three slightly different ways of doing this:

    (i) Producing a synonym.

    (ii) Giving a verbal definition or the *connotation* of the word.

    (iii) Using the word in a sentence in such a way that the sentence
could hardly make sense if any other word were substituted for it—
except of course an exact synonym if any exists. This may not be an
easy thing to do.

Use all three methods as far as you can to explain the meanings of:
*Bungalow, stupid, aeroplane, different, envious, various, green, precipice,
honourable, subtle*.

5. The sentence: 'A banana has a yellow skin' might be used to
explain:

    (i) what the word 'banana' means to someone who understands
'yellow' and 'skin';

    (ii) what the word 'yellow' means to someone who understands
'banana' and 'skin';

    (iii) what the word 'skin' means to someone who understands
'banana' and 'yellow'.

Discuss the extent to which the sentence is likely to be effective for
each of these three purposes.

6. You have in front of you an intelligent native of a little-known
South American tribe. You have at your disposal a wooden four-
legged table, a comfortable armchair, two buns, a pair of scissors and
the clothes you are now wearing. The native is clad only in a bright red
loin-cloth.

You know the following words in his language:

yumtifoo = pleasant, approved of
        iss = yes
urgipock = yesterday

Describe how you would attempt to explain to him the meanings of the following English words:

bit (noun), sideboard, comfortable, to know, many, money, usual, tomorrow.

Indicate in each case the extent to which you think your attempts are likely to be successful.

7. Comment on the Denotation and Connotation of the following: (i) Parallelogram, (ii) Mountain, (iii) Generosity, (iv) Jump, (v) Teacher, (vi) Honour, (vii) Centaur, (viii) Trousers, (ix) Uprightness, (x) John Smith.

8. Arguments are sometimes fallacious because the same word is used in different senses in the different stages of the argument. Discuss the extent to which this is so in the following passages:

(i) Knowledge is Power; Power corrupts; therefore Knowledge corrupts.

(ii) It is my duty to do all I can to promote the interests of those I love. The main interests of those I love at the moment are activities of which I heartily disapprove.

It is my duty therefore to encourage activities of which I heartily disapprove.

(iii) If ever a man was born with a silver spoon in his mouth it was Henry Higginbotham. All the comforts and luxuries of civilized life were bestowed upon him liberally by doting parents. He was liberally endowed by Providence with charm, intelligence and good looks. He received a liberal education. It followed necessarily therefore that he was a man who could be relied upon to take, in the widest sense, a liberal point of view on the pressing problems of the day.

(iv) The test suggested for whether an action is right is whether it promotes the welfare of the community. This sounds very nice and simple, but a difficulty arises because in any particular case we may have to decide whether the test has been rightly applied and in deciding whether the application is right we have to apply the same test as we used for the rightness of the original action.

(v) The view that the referee gets of a game is inevitably incomplete and partial; it is clearly impossible therefore to expect him to be impartial in his decisions.

9. 'Sometimes things may be made darker by definition. I see a *cow*; I define her, *Animal quadrupes ruminans cornutum*. But a goat ruminates, and a cow may have no horns. *Cow* is plainer.'

(Dr. Johnson, as reported by Boswell)

What is the point that Dr. Johnson seems to be making? Do you think he successfully makes it?

10. Comment on the emotive use of language in the following two letters, taken from the same copy of *The Times*:

'Sir,—Bromsgrove is to be commended for deciding to offer rewards to people who report offences against the Litter Act. If the enforcement of the Act were to be left entirely to policemen and park keepers there would be little chance of improving the disgraceful condition of our streets and open spaces. It is only with the help of public spirited men and women throughout the kingdom that the litter louts can be cured of their filthy habits. Reporting offenders will require considerable courage and should be given official support, both by the Home Office and by local councils.

Yours faithfully,'

'Sir,—I find it difficult to believe that any Bromsgrove parent will consent to his or her child being bribed to become that contemptible creature, a common informer.   Yours faithfully,'

11. Comment on the use of the words italicized in the following:

(i) 'All *real* men are gentle. Without tenderness, men are uninteresting.'

(Marlene Dietrich, *Daily Express*, 2 September, 1958)

(ii) 'The *freer* a work of art is in the bourgeois-anarchist sense, the less *free* it is in the Marxist sense and vice-versa.'

(Rude Pravo, quoted by *Observer*, 8 April, 1956)

12. 'The sublime is everything that is or will be so called by those who have employed or shall employ the name.'

(Benedetto Croce)

Do you think this is meant to be a definition? If not, what? Discuss.

13. Explain and comment on:

'For words are wise men's counters, they do but reckon by them: but they are the money of fools, that value them by the authority of an Aristotle, a Cicero or a Thomas, or any other Doctor whatsoever, if but a man.'

(Thomas Hobbes, *Leviathan*)

3

Propositions

WORDS are strung together to form sentences. Consider the following:

(1) Will you please shut the door.
(2) Present Arms.
(3) Where are the snows of yester-year?
(4) Is dinner ready?
(5) My aunt's pen is on the table.
(6) It's time to get up.
(7) I'll pay the butcher.
(8) All fish can swim.
(9) Some Englishmen like garlic.

These are all grammatical sentences, but they are of different forms and have very different functions to fulfil.

(1) is a request which is polite in form but might be said in such a tone of voice as to be exceedingly peremptory: it might express the last stages of exasperation with someone who has been consistently leaving doors unshut.

(2) is a command which is likely to be bellowed rather than spoken, and to be delivered in such a way as to be quite unintelligible to the uninitiated.

(3) and (4) are both questions, but of different kinds, and asked for different purposes. In any context in which one can imagine the question being asked the enquirer in (4) wants and expects an answer; but (3) looks like a poetical, rhetorical question and to

attempt to reply to it with a scientific explanation of what happens to snow when it melts would be felt by most people to be inappropriate. The questioner is probably reflecting on the general transitoriness of human affairs and does not expect his question to be answered.

(5), (6), (7), (8) and (9) are all statements, they assert something or they express a proposition. It is with sentences of this kind that we shall be mainly concerned.

STATEMENTS AND PROPOSITIONS

The sentences:

> My aunt's pen is on the table,
> The pen of my aunt is on the table,
> On the table is where my aunt's pen is,
> *La plume de ma tante est sur la table*,

are all different, but they all say or assert the same thing. A *proposition* means what is asserted, so that different sentences may state the same proposition.

The word 'statement' is used in both senses—the form of words of what is stated, and the content of what is stated—that is, it may mean either the sentence or the proposition. But whereas a sentence may be a question or a command and may not assert or state anything, a statement must always express some proposition.

Statements may have a different emphasis and assert something slightly different according to the context in which they occur. And to consider them apart from possible contexts is a dangerously misleading thing to do. 'My aunt's pen is on the table,' for example, might be said in answer to the question 'Where is your aunt's pen?' or in answer to the question 'What is that extraordinary looking object on the table?' or in answer to the request 'Please clear the table for lunch'—implying 'I'm sorry, but you know I'm not allowed to touch my aunt's things!' Which of these implications is intended will of course be clear not only from the context but also from the way in which the statement is made—the emphasis, the tone of voice.

The sentence 'It's time to get up' might be uttered by a lazy man lying in bed: the implication might be 'I *ought* to get up, but I'm not sure that I shall just yet': or it might be uttered by an energetic person standing beside the bed with one hand threateningly on the bed-clothes and the other brandishing a cold sponge, in which case it would be equivalent to the command 'Get out of bed'. So that although this sentence has the form of a simple statement it might be used with very different implications, and it might be used so as not to be a statement at all.

A statement or a proposition is the kind of thing that may be true or false. In particular cases it may be very difficult to say which, but it is always a sensible question to ask whether a proposition is true whereas it is never sensible to ask whether a question or a command is true.

There might be a difference of opinion as to whether the truth of the statement 'I'll pay the butcher' will only be determined in the future when it is seen whether I do pay the butcher, or whether it is true now if it expresses my genuine intention.

'All fish can swim' and 'Some Englishmen like garlic' are clear-cut, unequivocal statements and it is hard to imagine contexts for them in which they could be other than propositions which may be true or false.

It is with propositions of this kind that we are now going to deal.

PROPOSITIONS

Aristotle was the founder of the science of logic. He maintained that every proposition could be reduced to one of four kinds. We see now that this cannot satisfactorily be done, but his four propositional forms remain of some importance and they certainly cover many of the things which we want to assert. A study of them and of the way in which they are related is a valuable aid to clear thought, and provides some useful mental gymnastics.

Aristotle's four propositional forms are exemplified in the following sentences:

(1) All film stars are good-looking.
(2) No Frenchmen are cricketers.
(3) Some Socialists are rich.
(4) Some pillar-boxes are not red.

In each case there is a *Subject*, that about which something is asserted, i.e. film stars, Frenchmen, Socialists, pillar-boxes; a *Predicate*, that which is asserted or denied about the Subject, i.e. good-looking, cricketer, rich, red; and a *Copula*, which must be some part of the present tense of the verb 'to be'.

The Subject and the Predicate are called the terms of the proposition. Reference may be made to *all* or *some* of the subject-term; if the reference is to all the proposition is said to be *universal*, if only to some it is said to be *particular*. Thus (1) and (2) are universal propositions, (3) and (4) are particular. This is a difference in *quantity*. (1) and (3) are affirmative propositions, (2) and (4) are negative: this is said to be a difference in *quality*.

It is possible that there may be only one member of the subject term, (e.g. *this* apple which I hold in my hand; John Jones), in which case the proposition would normally be described as singular. It is easy to see, however, that such propositions can reasonably be described as universal; reference is made to *all* members of the class, but there is only one member. (It is true that there may be many people named 'John Jones', but there is only one member of the class 'John-Jones-to-whom-I-now-refer'.)

It is customary and useful to refer to these propositions in an abbreviated form. S and P are taken to stand for the Subject and Predicate respectively: '*a*', '*i*' stand for universal affirmative and particular affirmative respectively (the first two vowels of the Latin word *affirmo*), and '*e*', '*o*' stand for universal negative and particular negative respectively (the vowels of the Latin word *nego*).

Thus the Universal Affirmative 'all S is P' will be abbreviated as '$S \, a \, P$'.

'No S is P'   becomes $S \, e \, P$
'Some S is P'   becomes $S \, i \, P$
'Some S is not P' becomes $S \, o \, P$

A term is said to be 'distributed' if reference is made to all members of the class: it is 'undistributed' if reference is made to only some.

From what has already been said it is clear that the Subject is distributed in (1) and (2), and undistributed in (3) and (4). It is not so easy to see whether the Predicate is distributed.

If I say 'All film stars are good-looking' I am certainly not asserting that *only* film stars are good-looking: I am not saying in fact that all film stars comprise the whole class of good-looking people. The Predicate therefore is undistributed.

But when I say 'No Frenchmen are cricketers' I must mean to exclude the *whole* class of cricketers from the whole class of Frenchmen. The Predicate here therefore, is distributed.

The reader should now think out for himself whether the Predicate is distributed or undistributed in (3) and (4).

'SOME'

If I say 'Some pillar-boxes in Harlech are red' I would certainly be contradicted by the discovery that none were, and it might usually be thought that I would be contradicted by the discovery either that only one was red or that all of them were red.

In fact anyone who makes that statement probably uses the

word 'some' because he has seen two or three red ones but is not in a position to say that all are red, though he may not be excluding that possibility. It depends on the context in which, and the purpose for which, the statement is being made.

Probably the speaker would mean either: 'At least some,—i.e. more than one—are red: they may all be, but I don't know,' or, 'More than one is red but not all, because I've seen at least one blue one.' The intention in using 'some' is usually to exclude 'all', and it will often be clear from the context whether this is done from lack of information or because an exception is known.

In what follows, however, it is important to notice that in Aristotle's propositional forms, 'some' does not necessarily exclude all: it is used to mean 'one at least', that is any number from one to all inclusive.

EULER'S CIRCLES

If there are two classes of things or people—e.g. Frenchmen and cricketers—there are five possible relationships between them.

(1) They may be identical—i.e. all Frenchmen are cricketers, and all cricketers Frenchmen.

(2) They may overlap—i.e. some Frenchmen are cricketers and some are not, some cricketers are Frenchmen and some are not.

(3) The one may be completely included as a part of the other—i.e. all Frenchmen are cricketers, but not all cricketers are Frenchmen.

(4) The other may be completely included as a part of the one—i.e. all cricketers are Frenchmen but not all Frenchmen are cricketers.

5) They may be mutually exclusive—i.e. no cricketers are Frenchmen (from which it necessarily follows of course that no Frenchmen are cricketers).

These relationships may be very conveniently represented in diagrammatic form by circles ('*C*' and '*F*' stand for cricketers and Frenchmen). Thus:

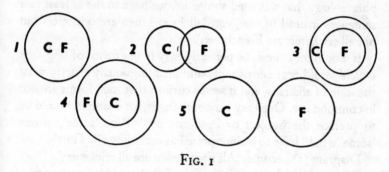

Fig. 1

These are usually called Euler's circles. It will be seen that these five cases exhaust *all* the possible relationships between cricketers and Frenchmen. Whenever there are two clearly defined classes of things it must be theoretically possible to represent the relationship between them by one of these diagrams.

It seems odd at first that the *A, I, E, O* forms do not, with one exception, correspond to the Euler's Circles diagrams. The exception is *S e P* (or, using cricketer and Frenchmen as Subject and Predicate, *C e F*), which corresponds unambiguously and uniquely with diagram 5. If it is true that 'no cricketers are Frenchmen' it is not possible for any of diagrams 1-4 to represent the state of affairs.

If, however, I say 'Some cricketers are Frenchmen' (or *C i F*) I might be describing the state of affairs represented by any one of the diagrams 1, 2, 3, 4 (remembering that 'some' is to be taken to mean 'one at least, perhaps all'). Similarly *C a F* can describe 1 or 4 and excludes 2, 3, 5; *C o F* describes 2, 3, 5 and excludes 1 and 4.

If we look at it, as it were, from the other end and want to describe in words the states of affairs represented by the diagrams we find, again, that only with number 5 can this be done simply and unambiguously. For the other four we have to use the sort of phraseology that was used above: i.e. we have to use at least two sentences instead of one, e.g. 'all Frenchmen are cricketers but not all cricketers are Frenchmen'.

It would, of course, be perfectly easy to use forms of language which would represent simply and unambiguously exactly what the state of affairs is, and it seems curious that such forms are not in common use. One easy way of doing it, for example, would be to preface the Subject or Predicate by 'all' or 'some', where 'some' would have to be interpreted as excluding all. Thus

Diagram (1) becomes 'All Frenchmen are all cricketers'.

Diagram (2) becomes 'Some Frenchmen are some cricketers'.

Diagram (3) becomes 'All Frenchmen are some cricketers'.

Diagram (4) becomes 'Some Frenchmen are all cricketers'.

Diagram (5) becomes 'No Frenchmen are cricketers'.

But even if sentences like this became customary we should certainly not want to use them always. It cannot be emphasized too often that whereas we want to be able to think and communicate accurately and precisely when it is necessary, and therefore we want to have words and forms of language which will enable us to do so, it is *not* always necessary. Our thinking and our talking are often intentionally vague, partly because we are not at the moment interested in greater precision and partly because we may not have the information that would enable us to be more precise. It is important to learn to be as accurate as you need to be for the purpose you are pursuing.

Suppose, for example, I say: 'Some Swiss hotels are over-crowded at Christmas.' This is a remark that might be made in a discussion or a comparing of notes about holidays. This says exactly as much, no more and no less, as I am interested in saying and am prepared to say. I know from experience and direct evidence that it is true. I do not want to specify, because I am not interested and do not know, whether *all* Swiss hotels are over-crowded. Nor am I interested for the purposes of the conversation in whether *all* the places that are overcrowded at Christmas are Swiss hotels, though if I were to reflect about it I would say it was unlikely. It is about 'Swiss hotels' that I wish to make a remark, not about 'places-that-are-overcrowded-at-Christmas'. This form of words, therefore, though in a sense it is vague, in that it admits any of diagrams 1, 2, 3, 4, is yet precisely suited to certain conversational purposes: precisely suited just *because* it is not too precise.

Notice that in the example just considered the two classes are both clear-cut, easily defined ones. It would not be difficult to enumerate members of the class 'Swiss hotels', though the enumeration might be rather a lengthy one. And it would be quite easy to define 'overcrowded' with fair precision in terms of numbers normally accommodated.

Consider another proposition: 'Some philosophers are absent-minded.'

Here again anyone making this statement would be unlikely to want to specify whether he includes *all* Philosophers and whether he thinks that there are some absent-minded people who are not Philosophers. But this proposition differs in an important respect from the one about Swiss hotels in that neither of the classes referred to is a clear-cut, easily defined one. We might define a Philosopher as anyone who now earns, or ever has earned, his living by the teaching or writing of Philosophy, and this would make the class a fairly clear-cut one though it might exclude some people who in the ordinary way we would call Philosophers.

The class of 'absent-minded people' is even more difficult. How absent does one's mind have to be? Most people are absent-minded sometimes. What *exactly* do we mean by absent-minded?

D

It seems that with this proposition it is awkward and misleading to think of it in terms of classes at all. What is being said is that there is a tendency for those whose minds are much occupied with elevated abstract thinking to be rather unpractical and distrait in everyday affairs. And if one were cross-examined as to exactly what was meant by the original statement that is the sort of way in which it would have to be rephrased.

Our ordinary forms of language are seen to correspond more closely with the things we usually want to say than do the Euler diagrams. But it still remains true that it would be useful to have simple sentences that correspond unambiguously with the diagrams, even though they might be used almost exclusively by logicians.

CONTRADICTORY AND CONTRARY

If you say 'That tree is an oak', and I say 'That tree is a beech', I would normally be said to have contradicted you. But 'Contradiction' in logic is used in a slightly different sense.

Two propositions are said to be contradictory if they can neither both be true together nor both be false together; one of them must be true and the other must be false.

The tree in question might be neither an oak nor a beech, so that we might both be wrong. The contradictory of 'That tree is an oak' is simply 'That tree is not an oak'.

'That tree is a beech' is said to be a *contrary* of 'That tree is an oak'.

Two propositions are said to be contrary if they cannot both be true together, but might be false together.

Notice that the above proposition has only got *one* contradictory—'That tree is not an oak,' but has many contraries—'That tree is a beech, an elm, a sycamore, a weeping willow, a figment of the imagination.'

The contradictory of a proposition is the simple denial of it:

'It is not true that . . .' or 'It is not the case that . . .'; but ambiguity may arise in some instances according to where the negative is inserted. If for example I want simply to deny the proposition: 'All Communists are scoundrels' I might say either 'Not all Communists are scoundrels' or 'All Communists are not scoundrels.' The second alternative might be held to mean the exclusion of every single Communist from the class of scoundrel, i.e. '*No* Communists are scoundrels', or it might merely mean the exclusion of at least one and it is this latter which is clearly meant by saying 'Not all Communists are scoundrels.' This is the proper contradictory, for the original statement is refuted by the discovery of a single Communist who is not a scoundrel. In fact a statement of the form 'All A's are not B's' would usually be taken to mean 'Not all A's are B's', though the latter way of putting it is to be preferred as being quite unambiguous. The contradictory of a negative proposition is clearly the corresponding affirmative proposition: the contradictory of 'Not all A's are B's' must be 'All A's are B's'; but the contradictory of 'No A's are B's' is not 'All A's are B's', but '*Some* A's are B's' where '*some*' might mean any number from *one* to *all*.

The four Aristotelian propositions can therefore be arranged in contradictory pairs:

'*S a P*' and '*S o P*' are contradictories of each other;

'*S e P*' and '*S i P*' are also contradictories of each other.

Notice that if two statements about A's and B's are contradictories, they must not only be incompatible with each other, but also they must between them exhaust *all* the possible relationships between A and B. Another way, therefore, of seeing that *S a P* and *S o P* are contradictories is to remind ourselves that *S a P* describes 1 or 4 of the Euler's Circles diagrams, and *S o P* describes the remaining three, 2, 3 or 5. Again *S e P* and *S i P* are contradictories because *S e P* describes diagram 5 and *S i P* describes 1, 2, 3 or 4.

In considering the proposition 'That tree is an oak' we said that it had only one contradictory, but many contraries. From what we have said above it should be obvious that every proposition has one and only one contradictory; we will now consider in more detail the situation about contraries.

If we think in terms of the diagrams, it is clear for example that diagram 1 is a contrary of diagram 5; they cannot both represent the state of affairs, but they might neither of them represent it. Similarly any two diagrams are contraries of each other, and any two propositions which are incompatible and which do not between them cover all the diagrams are contraries. Thus, $S \, a \, P$ and $S \, e \, P$ are contraries; for $S \, a \, P$ describes diagram 1 or 4, and $S \, e \, P$ describes only diagram 5. They might both be false for the true situation could be represented by diagram 2 or 3. Or putting it in words, we can see that 'All cricketers are Frenchmen' is a contrary of 'No cricketers are Frenchmen'; the true situation might be that some cricketers are Frenchmen. Other contraries of both these propositions may be obtained by specifying a definite number, e.g. '273 cricketers are Frenchmen', provided that this number is not that of all cricketers.

Further contraries of 'All cricketers are Frenchmen' are 'All cricketers are Germans, Esquimaux, Bohemians, Englishmen, etc.'. If we consider any one of these with the original they can clearly both be false together though they cannot both be true together. It should be noticed however, that in saying this we are assuming another proposition of the form 'No Frenchmen are Germans, Esquimaux, Bohemians, Englishmen, etc.'. If it were possible for Frenchmen also to be Esquimaux, 'All cricketers are Frenchmen', and 'All cricketers are Esquimaux', would not be contraries for they could theoretically both be true together.

$S \, i \, P$ does not have as a contrary any of the other three Aristotelian propositions $S \, a \, P, S \, e \, P, S \, o \, P$. It is easy to see this from the diagrams. For $S \, i \, P$ can represent any of the diagrams 1, 2, 3,

4, and the only proposition which could not be true with $S i P$, is $S e P$; this represents diagram 5, and therefore exhausts the possibilities and thus forms, as we have seen, its contradictory. Similarly $S o P$ has no contradictory among the other three main propositions.

If we look for a contrary to 'Some cricketers are Frenchmen', we will find that we can only get one by assuming some other proposition. 'All cricketers are Englishmen', for example, is a proposition which is incompatible with 'Some cricketers are Frenchmen', but does not exhaust the possibilities for all cricketers might be Esquimaux. But it assumes that no Frenchmen are Englishmen.

In other words no proposition merely about A's and B's is a contrary of 'some A's are B's'. If a third class, of C's, is introduced, and the assumption made that no C's are A's, then 'All B's are C's' becomes a contrary.

It is useful to know how the words *Contradictory* and *Contrary* are used in Logic, but we must re-examine with some caution what has been said about 'contradictory'. It is a good example of the danger that the study of Formal Logic may make one's thinking too rigid.

When we say that the contradictory of 'That tree is an oak' is 'That tree is not an oak' and that one of these statements must be true and the other false we assume, what in this case seems fairly obvious, that there is no other possibility, either it is or it isn't.

There is no difficulty here because what it is to be an oak-tree is well known and easily defined; every tree in the world is or is not an oak-tree and if we are experts in the subject we have no difficulty in saying which.

But suppose I say: 'That man is a cricketer'; the contradictory is 'That man is not a cricketer', and the assumption is that either he is or he isn't, there is no other possibility.

It is theoretically possible to define 'cricketer' in such a way that we could say of any man whether he is one or not, but it is certainly not a thing that anybody would be likely to want to do. We should probably have to draw the line so as to put on one side of it anybody who had ever played cricket, because that would be the most convenient place to draw it. But that would be to give the word a meaning which it does not ordinarily have— we usually mean 'keen on cricket', 'reasonably adept at cricket'.

As far as being a cricketer is concerned there are a very large number of gradations from the Test Match player to the club cricketer, to the schoolboy who just scrapes into a lowly school side, to the old lady who played once on the sand at Skegness, to the foreigner who has never even heard of the game. And the same is true of a great many other things in life.

'Either it is or it isn't' may be a very misleading thing to say and the danger of the Contradictory of Formal Logic is that it may make us think in terms of clear-cut distinctions where none are, in terms of black and white when in fact there are many intervening shades of grey. It is true that we can find propositions to which the clear-cut distinctions apply or can be made to apply by a suitable definition of the terms, and there is a danger that the logician will confine his attention to propositions of this kind. But the study of Logic is of value to us only if it helps us to deal with the thoughts and the propositions which arise in real life and it is important therefore to avoid artificiality and to remember that a two-valued logic of Yes and No, Black and White, has only a very limited field of application.

It is interesting and sometimes important, however, to consider whether we use certain pairs of words as contradictories or as contraries. If we talk about the over-50s and the under-50s for example it is clear that we intend to classify people in two mutually exclusive groups to one of which everybody must belong. These phrases are therefore contradictories: they are labels which cannot both be true of the same person and cannot both be false. The labels 'beautiful' and 'ugly', however, though they are certainly generally used in such a way that they cannot both be true, can perfectly well both be false: there are many people and things to which we would feel that neither epithet applied. These adjectives, therefore, are normally used as *contraries* and not as *contradictories*.

But it is important to realize that there are no hard and fast rules about this. In certain contexts and for certain purposes a pair of adjectives may be used as contradictories, on other occasions by someone else they may be used as contraries. Clearly the essential thing is to think about how we are using such adjectives ourselves and to try to judge from the context, when it is important to do so, how other people are using them.

EQUIVALENCE AND IMMEDIATE INFERENCE

If we know that no Englishmen are bull-fighters we also know that no bull-fighters are Englishmen: if we know that some beautiful people are thin we also know that some thin people are beautiful. These pairs of statements are called *equivalent*: they say exactly the same thing in words which are only slightly different.

We might also have pairs of statements which are not so obviously equivalent. If we assume that kind and unkind are contradictories, to say that all clever people are unkind is to say the same thing as that no clever people are kind. Again to say that all ripe tomatoes are red is equivalent to saying that some of the things which are red include the whole class of ripe tomatoes, or that no ripe tomatoes are not red, or that none of the things which are not red are ripe tomatoes. These statements will not add anything to the knowledge contained in the original statement, though they may be ways of expressing it which call attention to a different aspect of the matter and are therefore more convenient for some particular purpose.

These other ways of expressing a statement, especially when they are not so obviously equivalent to the original, are sometimes said to be derived from 'Immediate Inference'. We can also derive from Immediate Inference statements which say less than the original but whose truth is necessarily implied by the truth of the original. For example from the statement that *all* ripe tomatoes are red I am clearly entitled to infer that *some* ripe tomatoes are red, and in particular that this *one* ripe tomato which I am holding in my hand is red.

More important forms of Inference arise when two or more propositions are combined to produce new knowledge and these will be considered later.

EXAMPLE ON THE USE OF EULER'S CIRCLES

'In a certain community some of those who own television sets are members of the local Conservative Association, but no teetotallers are. Some teetotallers are not shopkeepers but all own television sets as do some shopkeepers. If "some" is to be interpreted as excluding "all", can you discover from this information whether there are any shopkeepers among the members of the local Conservative Association?'

Take V, C, T, S, to stand for owners of television sets, members of the local Conservative Association, teetotallers and shopkeepers respectively.

The relationship between V and C is

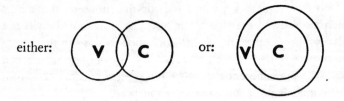

either: or:

As all T are V, but none are C, the complete facts about V, C and T are

either: (i) 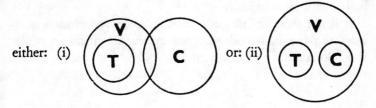 or: (ii)

Since some, but not all, S are V it would seem that the relationship between them could be represented thus:

But since we know that the T circle is completely enclosed by the V circle this would mean that all T are S, whereas in fact we know that some T are not S.

The S and V circles must therefore overlap thus:

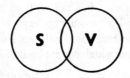

A similar argument shows that the S and T circles must do likewise.

The S circle can therefore be drawn in any position such that it cuts the V and T circles but does not enclose and is not enclosed by either of them.

It is easy to see that in both diagrams (i) and (ii) the circle could be drawn either to enclose C completely, or to cut it, or to lie completely outside it.

It is not therefore possible to come to any conclusion as to whether there are any shopkeepers among the members of the local Conservative Association.

Examples on Chapter 3

1. It was at one time claimed that every statement could be put into one of the *A, I, E, O* forms. This has been done with the sentences below, (not necessarily in the best possible way). Indicate in each case whether the revised version conveys the same meaning to you as the original: if not how would you improve it?

(i) 'Not all Conservatives are reactionary' becomes: 'Some Conservatives are not reactionary.'

(ii) 'I sometimes wonder whether you're mad' becomes: 'Some occasions are occasions when I wonder whether you're mad.'

(iii) 'Only those under 14 are allowed to travel at half-fare' becomes: 'No persons other than those under 14 are persons who are allowed to travel at half-fare.'

(iv) 'A man may play football without being expert at it' becomes: 'Some football-players are not expert football-players.'

(v) 'Few Englishmen have been to Russia' becomes: 'Some Englishmen are people who have not been to Russia.'

2. Examine the validity of the following argument. ('Some' is to be interpreted as *excluding* 'all'.)

'Some Socialists are opposed to Capital Punishment. Some people who are in favour of Capital Punishment are also in favour of Free Trade. All Liberals are in favour of Free Trade. Some Conservatives are in favour of Capital Punishment but no Conservatives are in favour of Free Trade. It therefore follows that some Socialists are in favour of Free Trade and that no Liberals are in favour of Capital Punishment.'

3. In a certain election there are five candidates A, B, C, D, E. It possible to vote for either one, two or three of them. You are given the following information:

All those who voted for A and all those who voted for B voted also for C. All those who voted for A voted for E. None of those who voted for B voted for either A or E. Some of those who voted for E did not vote for C. None of those who voted for D voted for C.

Discover, if possible, whether any of those who voted for D voted for A, B, or E.

4. The circles containing the letters A, B, C, D, E stand, in a certain society, for the classes of Aristocrats, Bald Men, Chess Players, Draughts Players and Ethiopians respectively. Express in words, as clearly and concisely as possible, the state of affairs represented by the diagram.

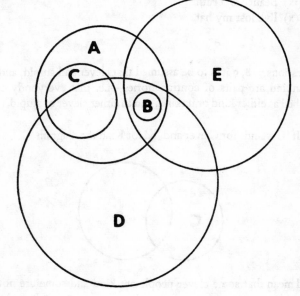

5. Discuss whether and in what contexts the following pairs of words are used as contradictories or as contraries: fast, slow; smooth, rough; fat, thin; clever, stupid; kind, unkind; reasonable, unreasonable; U, non-U.

6. Write down the contradictory and, where possible, one contrary of the following sentences: ('Some' is to be interpreted as *not* excluding all);

    (i) All Communists are knaves.
    (ii) Some express trains arrive on time.
    (iii) A stitch in time saves nine.
    (iv) No pigs can fly.
    (v) Some people are not honest about their Income Tax.
    (vi) It's a long lane that has no turning.
    (vii) Only Irishmen eat snails.
   (viii) What's sauce for the goose is sauce for the gander.
    (ix) Beauty is Truth.
    (x) I've lost my hat.

In questions 7, 8, 9 it is to be assumed that clever and stupid, and kind and unkind are pairs of contradictories—i.e. that everybody can be described as either kind or unkind, and as either clever or stupid.

7. If 'C' stands for Clever and 'K' for Kind the diagram

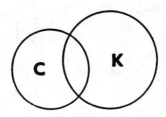

would mean that some clever people are kind and some are not, and that some kind people are clever and some are not. This state of affairs could also be represented by the diagram

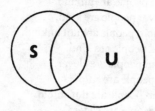

where 'S' stands for stupid and 'U' for unkind.

Represent similarly the situations represented by the diagrams:

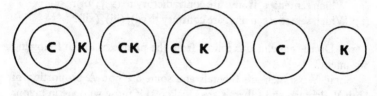

by diagrams which use only S and U.

8. Are the following pairs of sentences equivalent, contradictory, or contrary? ('Some' is to be interpreted as *not* excluding all.)

    (i) All kind people are stupid.
       No kind people are clever.
   (ii) Some clever people are unkind.
       All clever people are kind.
  (iii) Some unkind people are stupid.
       All unkind people are clever.
  (iv) All stupid people are kind.
       No kind people are stupid.
   (v) No stupid people are unkind.
       All kind people are clever.

9.   (i) All kind people are stupid.
     (ii) Some stupid people are unkind.

   (iii) No unkind people are clever.
   (iv) Some kind people are stupid.
    (v) All clever people are unkind.
   (vi) Some clever people are kind.
  (vii) Some stupid people are not unkind.
 (viii) No stupid people are kind.
   (ix) All unkind people are clever.
    (x) No kind people are stupid.
   (xi) Some kind people are not stupid.
  (xii) All kind people are clever.

(*a*) Which of the above sentences are equivalent to (i) or can be inferred from (i)?

(*b*) Which sentences, if any, are contradictory to (v), (vii)?

(*c*) Which sentences, if any, are contrary to (ii), (iii), (xii)?

10. Do the conclusions follow from the premisses in the following argument?

'Some Welshmen are Liberals and some are not. A proportion of both Welshmen and Liberals are Quakers. Of those who are in favour of lowering the school-leaving age none are Welshmen but some are Liberals. Some professional musicians are Welshmen and some are Quakers.

'It therefore follows that only a few of those who are in favour of lowering the school-leaving age can be Quakers and that some professional musicians are not in favour of lowering the school-leaving age.'

11. The membership of the Eccentrics Club is composed of all bald-headed men who are not members of the Oddities Club and all members of the Oddities Club who are not bald-headed. What can you say about membership of the Oddities Club?

4

Reasoning

JUST as words are strung together to form sentences so sentences may be strung together to form chains of reasoning. The links in such chains are usually words like 'if', 'then', 'since', 'therefore', 'because' and we have all studied and constructed such chains for ourselves many times. But we have become familiar with them gradually and we may not ever have paused to analyse closely exactly what is happening.

It will be convenient at this stage to introduce some examples in order to illustrate various distinctions and definitions.

(1) If you move your castle there I can take it with my knight.

(2) If Mrs. Jones sits next to Mrs. Smith they will probably quarrel.

(3) If you go out in the midday sun without a hat in some parts of the world you are likely to get sunstroke.

(4) Jones is a teetotaller and therefore he doesn't drink whisky.

(5) Since this figure is a parallelogram therefore its opposite sides are equal.

These are all elementary examples of reasoning of a type which every one of us uses frequently.

Let us consider them in more detail.

(1) 'If you move your castle there I can take it with my knight.' Assuming that this is true it is so because of the rules of chess and the positions of the pieces on the particular board we are talking about. The rules of chess might easily have been different but they are what they are, and starting from them as

given, one can arrive by chains of reasoning at conclusions, which are quite certain, as to the possible consequences of certain moves. In a piece of reasoning of this type the starting point, or that which is given, is called the *premiss* and that which is claimed to follow from it is called the *conclusion*. There may of course be more than one premiss and the premisses may be stated in words or they may be implied and taken for granted. In this case the stated premiss is my opponent moving his castle, the unstated premisses—unstated because they may be assumed to be known to both people taking part in the conversation—are the rules of chess and the positions of the pieces on the board. The conclusion is 'I can take it (your castle) with my knight'.

This particular bit of reasoning takes place in what we might call a *closed* system of thinking. Once the rules of chess, including the ways in which the pieces move, are understood, nothing from outside can alter the certainty of the conclusion. It is not possible that someone should come along and say that he's just found a knight that moves differently and which would therefore *not* be able to take your castle. Or rather if such a person did come along the complete and final answer to be made to him would be 'That's very interesting, but it's not chess'.

This kind of reasoning is called *Deduction*. As the Latin derivation of the word implies it is a process of 'drawing out' what is already there in the premisses. In a closed system such as chess the conclusions, if correctly drawn, follow necessarily and are quite certain. But it should be noticed that there is nothing very wonderful about that for *we* put the certainty there by making the rules.

(2) 'If Mrs. Jones sits next to Mrs. Smith they will probably quarrel.' This proposition is of a very different kind. The premiss here is Mrs. Smith and Mrs. Jones sitting next to each other, and the conclusion is their probable disagreement. If this reasoning is to have any validity it must be based on the speaker's past experi-

ence of the ladies concerned, what they have said about
other, their tendency to be quarrelsome, and the results of th
associations in the past. The system here is certainly not a *closed*
one as in the example about the chess players. If Mrs. Brown
comes along and says that she knows for a fact that Mrs. Smith
and Mrs. Jones have patched up their past disagreement and are
now the greatest friends in the world, this would certainly be a
very relevant piece of evidence which might cause us to decide
that the conclusion no longer followed from the premiss. This
reasoning takes place in an *open* system where what is happening
in the outside world may continually be making a difference,
introducing new premisses or altering old ones, stated or unstated.

In this case whether Mrs. Brown's evidence makes us come to
a different conclusion or not, the important point to note is that
the conclusion is or should be drawn because of many particular
bits of evidence in the past which have enabled the speaker to
form a general estimate of the characters of Mrs. Smith and Mrs.
Jones. This process of reasoning is called *Induction*: it is a process
in which one is arguing from experience, from evidence supplied
by the outside world in an open system. A general rule which is
formed from particular cases, that is a rule formed by Induction,
can never have the same kind of certainty as the conclusions
arrived at by Deduction in a closed system, though it may have
a very high degree of probability.

I regard it as virtually certain for example that the sun will set
tonight but it is not a certainty of the same kind as that a knight's
move in chess is what it is. The second is certain *now* by definition, it follows necessarily from the premisses; for the first we
have to wait and see what happens. It is worth noticing also that
the adjective *certain* is applied either to our states of mind as in
'I am certain that . . .' or to a proposition independently of our
mental attitude to it as in 'It is certain that . . .'. The first kind of

E

...d psychological or subjective certainty, and ... be called objective certainty. We shall have ... ut the distinction between these two and ...tainty of inductive processes.

...n the midday sun without a hat in some ... world you are likely to get sunstroke.' This sentence is a straightforward piece of *Induction*. From evidence in the past, personal experience, hearsay, or what he has read, the speaker is inducing a general rule—though it might be argued that without being rather more specific about where 'some parts of the world' are it is not a very useful one. He is certainly arguing from experience of particular cases and the system of reasoning in which he is operating is certainly an open one. A Professor might come along and say that he has discovered an ointment or a pill which will enable one to go out in the midday sun in any part of the world without a hat and without getting sunstroke.

More items of evidence derived from testing the Professor's claim might or might not lead to an alteration in the general rule, or to the degree of probability to be attached to it.

(4) 'Jones is a teetotaller and therefore he doesn't drink whisky.' This might be interpreted in such a way as to be hardly a piece of reasoning at all. It might be argued that Jones does not refrain from drinking whisky *because* he is a teetotaller, but that he is a teetotaller because amongst other things he does not drink whisky. In other words part of the definition of a teetotaller is not drinking whisky. It is rather like saying 'that animal is a quadruped *therefore* it has four legs'.

But it is more likely that the sentence is intended to express the fact that his not drinking whisky is derived from a general principle which he has formed not to drink anything containing alcohol. This principle might have been formed on grounds of religion, economy, or at the request of some relation.

Or it may happen that he just does not like whisky and having

tasted other spirits, wines, beer and all liquids which co[ntain]
alcohol, he finds that he does not like them either. He is theref[ore]
in a sense, a teetotaller and though it would be more proper t[o]
say that it is *because* he does not drink whisky (and other things)
that he is a teetotaller, rather than the other way round, the sentence might still be used of him by someone who is 'explaining'
why he will not have a drink.

While the word was originally used to describe someone who
refrains on principle and is probably still used more often in that
sense, it is now sometimes employed—'incorrectly' as many
people would claim—to describe the fact without implying a
reason for it.

(5) 'Since this figure is a parallelogram therefore its opposite
sides are equal.' This is a straightforward example of a piece of
deductive reasoning in a closed system. Starting from the definition of a parallelogram (a quadrilateral with both pairs of opposite sides parallel), and assuming various definitions and axioms
about straight lines and parallels, it can be demonstrated by a
chain of reasoning, with which most readers are probably familiar, that the opposite sides are equal. This sentence is merely the
statement of the initial premiss in a compressed form and of the
final conclusion. The intermediate steps are omitted and no one
could be expected to appreciate the validity of the reasoning unless he had been taken through these intermediate steps or had
had an opportunity to work them out for himself.

All these sentences have so far been considered apart from the
particular contexts in which they might have been said or written.
In fact if they are real pieces of thinking used by real people communicating with each other they must have a context and it may
be very misleading to consider them in isolation. For certain purposes it may be necessary, (the people who do it are usually
Philosophers, Logicians, Linguists or writers of books on
'The Use of Reason') but it must be done with great caution. We

hole time of an actual or possible context in
any conclusions which are claimed to follow
of such sentences in isolation must be re-

r example, might be uttered by someone
......ng a friend to play chess and is at the moment of
speaking showing him how a knight moves. He would indicate
that such was his intention by his tone of voice, the way in which
he stressed the words or the pauses he made. In order to convey
this emphasis in writing it would be necessary to rephrase the
sentence: 'A knight's move is such that if the castle is moved to
this square' (which could be described in the notation generally
used by chess-players) 'this knight would be able to take it.'

Our previous analysis in which we described it as a piece of
deductive reasoning from the premisses, assumed to be known,
of the ways in which the pieces moved, the rules of chess, and the
particular position on the board, would then be misleading and
would not accurately describe the purpose for which the sentence
was being used. The conclusion which it was intended to convey
was one which we assumed to be in the premisses.

The second sentence, regrettably, might have been uttered
with the intention of vilifying Mrs. Jones and/or Mrs. Smith (it
may be none the less true) and any useful examination of this
sentence would certainly have to take that into account.

The reader will be able to think for himself of ways in which
the other sentences might have been used, or contexts from which
they might have been taken, which would render the analysis that
has been given earlier at least misleading.

DEDUCTION AND INDUCTION

We have seen that sentences (1) and (5) are examples of deductive reasoning, while (2) and (3) are inductive.

It is sometimes said that deduction is the process of reasoning from general rules to other general rules or to particular cases, and that induction is the building up of a general rule from many particular cases. But this is only a partial account. Deduction certainly includes arguing from the general to the particular, but it also includes any case when one is *drawing out* what is in the premisses, or analysing the premisses to form a conclusion. Deductive reasoning is therefore sometimes called *analytic*.

Similarly statements which are entirely self-contained and merely tell us something about how the words or the symbols in the sentence are to be used are said to be *analytic*. For example 'A quadrilateral is a four-sided figure' is obviously merely giving us the definition of the word 'quadrilateral'. It is perhaps less obvious that the statement '3 + 7 = 10' is analytic, but if one understands the terms and symbols involved the statement is merely drawing out or analysing what is already there; though it would not be true that '3 apples added to 7 apples produces a pile of 10 apples' is analytic for that is a statement about the real world outside us and though it is true of apples it would not be true of everything, for example drops of water.

Statements about the real world, derived from experience, are sometimes called *empirical*. Most of the statements we make are of this kind, though it will sometimes be difficult but rather important to decide whether a statement in a given context is intended to be analytic or empirical. If someone says, for example, 'All right-minded people are in favour of a more even distribution of wealth' this might be interpreted as either. If it is analytic it is simply a definition of what it is to be right-minded; but if it is empirical the classification of 'right-minded' people must have been made on other grounds, and the statement is a claim that all those so classified would express themselves in favour of a more even distribution of wealth, and one person who failed to do so would disprove the statement.

An aid to deciding whether a statement is intended to be

analytic or empirical may sometimes be to consider whether it can be verified or falsified, and if so how. If the above statement is analytic it can neither be verified nor falsified: it is true by definition. The questioning of a large number of people will merely enable the questioner to decide to which of them the label 'right-minded' can properly be attached. If, however, the statement is empirical the question need only be put to those who already bear the label 'right-minded'; if any one of them gives a negative answer the statement is immediately falsified; for it to be verified all of them must answer Yes. This illustrates the fact that falsification is much simpler than verification; the latter process can in many cases never be completed.

In fact, of course, the statement is likely to mean something like this: 'I am in favour of a more even distribution of wealth and I cannot understand anyone who thinks about the matter at all disagreeing with me.' In which case it might be said that the statement is neither analytic nor empirical but merely expresses the attitude of the speaker.

Induction is concerned with empirical statements, and as we have seen it includes the process of reasoning from particular cases to a general rule. But though it is always an argument from particular cases the reasoning need not always lead to a general rule. Because inductive reasoning is a process of 'putting together' it is sometimes called *synthetic*.

If, starting from Euclidean axioms about straight lines, I prove that the three angles of any triangle add up to two right-angles and I then go on to say that the three angles of this particular triangle which I have in front of me therefore add up to two right-angles, my reasoning is entirely deductive. But it is possible that the rule might have been formed by taking a large number of particular triangles measuring their angles and finding that the total always seemed to be approximately 180 degrees. To do this would be to form the general rule by induction, but this method could clearly not give either the certainty (might there not be some triangle somewhere whose angle-sum was different?), or the precision (perhaps the total of the angles of every triangle is $179° 59'$?). In fact the method of induction is not used at all in Geometry; the general rules are all formed by deduction from the basic axioms which are man-made definitions and are therefore artificial in the same way as the rules of chess are artificial, though less obviously so.

The methods of the physical sciences, however, are obviously almost entirely inductive. The 'laws' which are formulated by scientists are derived from many particular instances and are therefore formed by a process of induction. But once they have been formed further particular conclusions may be *deduced* from them.

A distinction is usually drawn between branches of knowledge which are Inductive, that is open systems in which the rules are formed by Induction (for example Physics, Chemistry, Mechanics, Psychology); and branches which are Deductive, that is closed systems in which the rules are arbitrary laws (as in chess), or man-made definitions, or deductions from other rules (for example Pure Mathematics, Symbolic Logic).

There may sometimes be disagreement as to the extent to which a branch of knowledge should be inductive—i.e. based on experiment and observation, or deductive—i.e. derived from basic general principles. Political Philosophy, for example, which was once thought of as mainly deductive is being increasingly regarded as inductive as is implied by the fact that it is now called a Social Science.

'A PRIORI' AND 'A POSTERIORI'

Other epithets which are sometimes applied to reasoning to distinguish between that which is deductive and that which is inductive are '*a priori*' and '*a posteriori*'. Deductive reasoning is called '*a priori*' because it starts from general principles which are regarded as logically prior to the particular facts which exemplify them or, in a sense, follow from them. Inductive reasoning is called '*a posteriori*' because it starts from the facts which are dependent on or posterior to the principles.

Into many chains of reasoning both the deductive and inductive processes enter. If we want to decide which process is being used it is often helpful to consider the kind of evidence we should require to test their validity.

VALIDITY

We talk about the reasoning being *valid* and about the premisses or conclusions being *true*. It is important to notice that the reasoning may be valid though the premisses and conclusions are both false, and that the reasoning may be invalid though the premiss and conclusion are both true. Valid reasoning from a true premiss, however, must lead to a true conclusion. Invalid reasoning from a true premiss may or may not lead to a false conclusion.

How do we recognize whether the reasoning is valid or not? The best way to answer this is by considering some examples.

Suppose that A, B, C, stand for quantities (e.g. sums of money, numbers of people, etc.), then if $A = B$ and $B = C$ we may validly deduce that $A = C$. Once we know what is meant by 'quantity' and by 'is equal to' we cannot fail to agree that the inference is valid. If A and C really are both equal to B, then we find it impossible to conceive of their not being equal to each other. And if we find someone who is not convinced, we think that either he has failed to understand the terms involved or he is not quite right in the head. We feel *certain* because we are unable to conceive its not being true: we see that it follows *necessarily*, and perhaps 'necessary' is a more appropriate word to apply to the conclusion than 'certain'.

It should be noticed that our appreciation of the validity of this reasoning depends on our *understanding* the terms involved. When reasoning becomes more difficult it is often not because the steps to be taken are harder, but because it requires much more knowledge, experience and perhaps subtlety of thought to understand the terms involved and their various properties.

Let us consider now how we judge the validity of a piece of inductive reasoning.

Consider this proposition: 'If you drink a pint of prussic acid you will immediately die in horrible agony', and suppose that this is a remark made to a particular person at a particular time. The implication clearly is that you will die in horrible agony because of, as a result of, drinking the prussic acid; and that this is a particular case of a general rule: 'Anyone (i.e. any human being) who drinks a pint of prussic acid will, as a result, die immediately in horrible agony.'

It is a statement of cause and effect. How are we to judge whether this cause and this effect are validly (i.e. invariably and necessarily) connected? Putting aside for the moment the possibility of trying the experiment ourselves, we should want to have examples quoted to us. How many known cases are there? What is the evidence? Who saw it happen? Is there any single case known of someone drinking a pint of prussic acid and not dying in horrible agony? We judge the validity of the reasoning (i.e. the connection of the cause and effect) by examining the nature of the evidence; and to be convinced that there is a necessary connection we should want to be shown that in every known case where the cause has operated the effect has followed.

It would be hard to feel quite certain in this case. Might there not be a man somewhere who was so tough by nature or training that he would not be affected in this way by prussic acid? In any case it is not *inconceivable* that that should be so. I can have a mental picture of a man drinking a bottle of prussic acid and rather enjoying it. But I am unable to form a mental picture of

quantities *A* and *B* both being equal to *C* and yet not being equal
to each other.

(It is true that a scientist who is better acquainted with the
terms involved—the nature of prussic acid and the nature of the
human interior—may well say that it is inconceivable that it
should be otherwise. But one could retaliate by saying that at any
rate one can conceive a world where it is not true, whereas one
cannot conceive a world where if $A = B$ and $B = C$, *A* is not
equal to *C*.)

In a process of Deduction, then, as applied to mathematical or
closed systems, we become convinced that the reasoning is valid
when, understanding the terms and definitions involved, we see
that it follows necessarily or we find it inconceivable that the
conclusion should be otherwise.

The validity of a process of Induction, however, is a much
more uncertain and relative affair. It is a statement of cause and
effect and we judge the necessity of their connection and therefore the validity of the reasoning by an examination of the
evidence and perhaps, if we have the opportunity, by making
experiments.

SOME EXAMPLES CONSIDERED

Let us consider the kind of evidence we should require for the
validity of chains of reasoning where it is less obvious whether
they are deductive or inductive.

Consider the following:

> *If an action is cruel it is unjustifiable.*

In order to test this would we go and do a few cruel actions
and see whether they turned out to be justifiable? Obviously not.
But we would think of real or imaginary cruel actions and try to
decide whether there are circumstances in which they might be
justified. In deciding this we would to a large extent be reflecting
on just how we use the words 'cruel' and 'justifiable', and we

would also be applying our general moral principles. Our thinking, in fact, would be made up of three elements—examining particular cases, analysing the way in which words are used, application of general rules.

If you eat too many sweets you will be ill.

Shall we test this by going and eating too many sweets and seeing whether we become ill? But how many sweets is too many? Obviously the number that will make us ill. In other words as soon as we analyse this the conclusion is so obviously contained in the premiss that we should hardly describe it as a piece of reasoning at all. In any context in which it is likely to be used the meaning it is intended to convey is almost certainly: 'Mind you don't eat so many sweets that you become ill.'

If wages are increased prices will rise.

Shall we go and raise a few wages and see whether prices rise? Unfortunately it is not as simple as this, for it would be impossible for us to make the experiment on a large enough scale to be any good; and even if we could, the network of cause and effect in Economics is so complicated that it is very difficult indeed to trace any particular event (for example a rise in prices) to any single cause. This sentence might be uttered by a Managing Director who is resisting a request for increased wages, in which case it might certainly be valid because it is the expression of an intention ('If I grant you higher wages I shall have to put up prices'). But if it is the statement of a general rule we would test its validity by examining statistics to see whether an increase in wages is always accompanied by a rise in prices and we would study the general principles of Economics. We would probably come to the conclusion that though an increase in wages is one of the factors, and a very important one, which tend to make prices rise one is not justified in stating it as a universal rule.

Prejudice is a mixture of pride and egotism, and no prejudiced man therefore will be happy.

(Lord Beaverbrook, *Daily Express*, 25 August, 1955)

What tests shall we make here? In the first place we can simplify it a little by agreeing not to question the way in which the writer is using the word 'prejudice'. This word can easily be cut out so that what is being said is equivalent to: 'No person in whom there is a mixture of pride and egotism will be happy.' We have then got to think carefully how we use the words 'pride' and 'egotism'. And perhaps the easiest way of doing that is to try to think of people to whom we would apply the adjectives 'proud' and 'egotistic'. This is not very easy, partly because being proud is a matter of degree—most of us are proud to some extent—and partly because it is used in rather different senses. Proud of what—my family, my country, my achievements, or myself? But the writer probably means proud in the sense of 'haughty' and egotistic in the sense of 'self-centred'. Are such people happy? It's rather difficult to tell: they put up such a barrier. But in fact the ones I know do seem to me to be rather happy.

Different people will come to different conclusions about this: the important thing is the method of testing the validity of the reasoning.

(It is perhaps possible that the writer meant that as pride and egotism were qualities of which he did not approve no one who was proud and egotistic *ought* to be happy. But that is not what he appears to be saying.)

Examples on Chapter 4

1. Complete the following table (in some cases the answer may be indeterminate):

PREMISS	REASONING	CONCLUSION
True	Valid	
True	Invalid	
Untrue	Valid	
Untrue	Invalid	
True		True
True		Untrue
Untrue		True
Untrue		Untrue

In each case construct simple sentences to illustrate your answer.

2. Consider whether the following statements are analytic or empirical or neither. It will be a help if you think how you would verify or falsify them. (There are not necessarily clear-cut answers: if you think it depends on the context you should say so.)

(i) A quadruped has four legs.

(ii) A cow has two ears.

(iii) Good men do not seek after pleasure.

(iv) All dangerous drivers drink.

(v) Gravity is what makes bodies fall to the ground.

(vi) Beauty is Truth, Truth Beauty.

(vii) Money is the root of all evil.

(viii) 'No man is born into the world whose work is not born with him.'

(ix) Honesty is the best policy.

(x) Genius is an infinite capacity for taking pains.

(xi) Courage is the most important virtue.

(xii) 'Our reserves remain pitiably inadequate, the national economy is frozen in a rigid mould and the weapons for controlling it are rusty, blunt and antiquated.'

(xiii) It will snow here next week.

(xiv) It will rain or not rain here to-morrow.

3. Discuss the extent to which the following pieces of reasoning are deductive or inductive. Consider in each case how you would test their validity.

(i) If you are badly taught you are not likely to pass your examinations.

(ii) If Tommy is older than Barbara and Barbara is older than Kate, then Kate is younger than Tommy.

(iii) If you bathe in this weather you will catch your death of cold.

(iv) No newspaper can be great unless it represents a cause.

(v) If people go to bed early and rise early they become healthy, wealthy and wise.

(vi) If more factories close down there will be more unemployment.

(vii) If one side of a triangle is produced the exterior angle so formed is equal to the sum of the interior opposite angles.

4. The following is a 'Proposition' from *Mathematical Principles of Theology* by Richard Jack (published in 1747):

'*Any being, whose existence is independent of another being, may exist without the existence of that other being.*'

'Let A and B be any two beings, and let the existence of the being A, be independent of the being B.

'I say, that A may exist without the existence of B: For A may either exist without the existence of B, or not. If the being A cannot exist without the existence of B, then because any being that cannot exist without the existence of some other being, its existence is dependent on that other being: therefore the existence of A is dependent of B, which is absurd. Wherefore the being A can exist without the existence of the being B.

'Therefore, any being, whose existence is independent of another being, may exist without the existence of that other being, which was to be demonstrated.'

Discuss whether the statement of the proposition is analytic or empirical. Is the reasoning contained in the 'Proof' deductive or inductive? Comment on its validity.

5. Are there any unstated premisses in the following pieces of reasoning? If so, what are they? Discuss the validity of the arguments.

(i) 'The Irish are a Fair People; they never speak well of one another.'

(Dr. Johnson as reported by Boswell)

(ii) 'Yes, I agree. But perhaps I can convince you what a wonderful chap he is by pointing out that all that glitters is not gold.'

(iii) 'It is surely inconceivable that the Tories should lose the next election unless the nation as a whole is suddenly bereft of the last glimmerings of good sense.'

5

Compound Propositions

In the last chapter we considered some simple examples of reasoning, and we saw that conclusions could be arrived at either by induction or deduction or by some combination of both.

We are now going to undertake a more formal and a more exhaustive examination of propositions of the type—'If . . . then. . . .' These are called *hypothetical* sentences.

Consider the proposition:

(1) 'If the sides of a triangle are in the ratio 3 : 4 : 5 then the triangle is right-angled.'

This is an elementary geometrical fact which we know to be true. The condition of having sides in the ratio 3 : 4 : 5 is *sufficient* to ensure that the triangle is right-angled. But it is not *necessary*. We know that if the sides are in the ratio 5 : 12 : 13 or 7 : 24 : 25 the triangle is also right-angled. The condition is one without which the conclusion may very well be true.

Consider another proposition:

(2) 'If 2 angles of a triangle are equal then the triangle is isosceles.'

This, again, we know to be true and it follows therefore that the condition is *sufficient*. But here the condition is also *necessary*. In order that the conclusion (of being isosceles or having 2 sides equal) shall be true it is essential that 2 angles should be equal. The condition is one without which the conclusion cannot be true.

We might also express this fact by saying that with the second proposition the converse is also true ('If a triangle is isosceles then two of its angles are equal'), whereas the converse of the first proposition ('If a triangle is right-angled then its sides are in the ratio 3 : 4 : 5') is not true.

It will be convenient at this stage to introduce a simple notation. We shall use letters '$p, q, r \ldots$' to stand for simple propositions of the type 'the triangle is right-angled' and we shall denote their contradictories thus '$\bar{p}, \bar{q}, \bar{r} \ldots$'.

The compound propositions with which we are dealing can therefore be represented generally by 'If p, then q', 'If $\bar{p}$, then $\bar{q} \ldots$', etc.

By considering particular propositions about triangles we saw that if the proposition 'If p, then q' is true then p must state a condition *sufficient* for the truth of q but it need not state a condition which is *necessary* for the truth of q: i.e. it is possible, as in the example about the right-angled triangle, for q to be true without p being true.

If the condition is sufficient *and* necessary then p and q must both be true together and both be false together.

If, however, p states a condition which is *necessary* but not *sufficient* for the truth of q then of course the proposition 'If p, then q' is not true, for if it were true the condition would have been sufficient. Consider for example:

(3*a*) 'If a number is even it is divisible by 4.'

Here the proposition is clearly not true: a number being even is a *necessary* condition for its divisibility by 4, but it is not a *sufficient* one. But of course if we state it the other way round (its converse) (3*b*) 'If a number is divisible by 4, then it is even', we clearly get a true proposition.

Now that we have seen what necessary and sufficient conditions are, it should be obvious that if p states a necessary (but not sufficient) condition for q, then q states a sufficient (but not necessary) condition for p, and that if p states a sufficient (but not necessary) condition for q, then q states a

F

necessary (but not sufficient) condition for *p*. Clearly if *p* states a necessary *and* sufficient condition for *q*, then *q* states a sufficient *and* necessary condition for *p*.

When we say 'If *p*, then *q*' the condition *p* may or may not be necessary (though it must clearly be sufficient). We are therefore not entitled to infer from 'If *p*, then *q*', 'If *q*, then *p*'.

'If *p*, then *q*' means that from the truth of *p* the truth of *q* must follow. If *q* is not true, therefore, then *p* cannot be true, either, for if it were then *q* would be true.

From 'If *p*, then *q*' we can therefore deduce 'If *q̃*, then *p̃*'.

From sentence 3*b*, for example, we can clearly deduce that 'If a number is not even then it is not divisible by 4.' It is sometimes said that 'If *q̃*, then *p̃*', and 'If *p*, then *q*' are *equivalent* propositions, i.e. are different ways of saying the same thing, and it is sometimes said that the one can be inferred or deduced from the other.

'EITHER ... OR ...'

Propositions of the form 'If *p*, then *q*' are sometimes expressed in other ways.

A schoolmaster who wants to issue the warning: 'If you go on doing that you will be punished,' may say instead: 'Either you stop doing that or you will be punished.' The second sentence, with the emphasis on *stopping*, may act as a more effective warning because it is likely to be uttered in such a way as to be more nearly a command. But the two sentences express the same piece of reasoning: in both cases the speaker is saying that from a certain course of action certain consequences will follow. In the first sentence 'going on doing that' is stated to be a sufficient condition for being punished, though it might be claimed that there is no implication that it is a necessary one: it would be possible for the person addressed to stop 'doing that' and yet to be punished for something quite different. If, however, he did stop and were still punished for 'doing that' the punisher would be likely to be accused of sharp practice and unfairness. Although he could say with some justification 'I never said that if you didn't go on doing that you would not be punished', that is the implication that most people would read into his words.

The 'Either . . . or . . .' way of saying it seems to express that implication even more clearly. In order to ensure that 'going on doing that' is not interpreted as a *necessary* condition for being punished, i.e. that he may be punished even if he doesn't go on doing that, the speaker would have to say 'Either you stop doing that or you will be punished, or both.' This would certainly remove much of the force and effectiveness of the sentence and is not a thing that would normally be said.

If, however, we do understand 'Either p or q' to include 'or both' it becomes logically equivalent to 'If p, then q'. It is called the *alternative* form of the sentence.

Almost always, however, when we use 'either . . . or . . .' we mean to exclude both, and it is usually just because we have this intention that we select this way of expressing our thought. It is a way of emphasizing 'but not both'.

This will be seen more clearly by considering some examples:

    (i) Either you move your king there or you'll be mated next move.

    (ii) Either that tree is a beech or it's an oak.

    (iii) Either my hat is in the cloakroom or I must have left it in the garden.

    (iv) We must export or die.

    (v) Either a triangle has not got sides which are in the ratio of $3 : 4 : 5$ or it is right-angled.

    (vi) Either it is or it isn't.

    (vii) Either that animal has not got wings or it's not a cow.

    (viii) Either it's squameous or it's a grifficorn.

(ix) Either you doldefy the grumptions or the crum will hallify.

In numbers (i), (ii), (iii), and (vi), the implication is clearly 'but not both'. Let us see how they look if we change them into the 'if . . . then . . .' form; thus:

(i) 'If you don't move, your king there, then you'll be mated next move.'

(ii) 'If that tree is not a beech, then it's an oak.'

(iii) 'If my hat is not in the cloakroom, then I must have left it in the garden.'

(vi) 'If it is not, then it isn't.'

(i), (ii), (iii) are statements which it would only be sensible to make if, in the particular context, the condition were intended to be *necessary* as well as sufficient. 'Not moving your king there' must surely be here a necessary condition for being mated: the advice to the chess player (perhaps to one's opponent) would indeed be heartless unless the implication were that if you do move your king there you will avoid being mated next move.

It is even more obvious that the implications of (ii) and (iii) must be that if that tree *is* a beech then it's not an oak, and that if my hat *is* in the cloakroom then I cannot have left it in the garden. (It may be worth reminding the reader that the simplest way of thinking whether 'p' states a *necessary* condition for 'q' is by considering whether $\bar{p}$ states a *sufficient* condition for $\bar{q}$, i.e. whether 'If $\bar{p}$, then $\bar{q}$' is true.)

The revised form of (vi) needs no further comment.

In number (iv) it can certainly be said that if the sentence is to be taken literally 'or both' can be added, for whether we export or not we must all die some time. But the sentence is clearly to some extent metaphorical and expressed in an exaggerated way to drive home a point—namely the importance of our export trade to our survival as a nation. If pressed, the speaker would probably admit that exporting might not guarantee survival, in other words that not exporting is only a *sufficient* condition for dying and need not be a necessary one; or he might prefer to put it the other way and say that exporting is a necessary condition for survival though it may not be a sufficient one. In any case whether it is sufficient is not the point, what he is saying is that it is *necessary*.

We know that in numbers (v) and (vii) it is possible and true to add 'or both'. We have already seen that it is possible for a triangle not to have sides which are in the ratio 3 : 4 : 5 and yet be right-angled. And it is certainly possible for an animal not to have wings and yet not to be a cow. But we know that we can add 'or both' because of our acquaintance with triangles, right-angles, animals, wings and cows, and not from any other considerations. When we come to consider sentences (viii) and (ix) we have no idea at all whether it would be right to add 'or both'. We have not been taught what it is to be squameous or a grifficorn; we have no experience of doldefying grumptions and we have never seen a crum hallify.

The point of course is that when we consider examples with whose terms we are acquainted, we decide whether it would be right to add 'or both'. From an accumulation of such examples we see whether the form of words 'either . . . or . . .' is or is not normally used to include 'or both' and we then use this know-ledge to see what is likely to be meant when the terms are un-familiar.

Experience of the written and spoken word would seem to show that (v) and (vii) would today be considered very odd and even misleading ways of saying: 'If a triangle has sides which are in the ratio of 3 : 4 : 5 then it is right-angled,' and: 'If an animal has got wings then it's not a cow.' The implication of (v) for most people who do not already know about right-angled tri-angles would surely be that all triangles can be arranged in two piles: in the first pile we put all those which have not got sides in the ratio 3 : 4 : 5 and in the second all those which are right-angled, and these two piles are mutually exclusive.

In examples in which 'Either . . . or . . .' is used to express a causal or logical link, e.g. in (i), (iv), (v) above, the sentences can usually be more effectively rephrased in the form 'If not . . . then . . .'. Let us consider two more examples where it is used to express a simple alternative.

(x) I shall catch either the 8.23 or the 8.47.

(xi) The date is either the 7th or the 8th.

The first sentence might imply 'but I haven't yet made up my mind', or it might imply 'I want to catch the 8.23, but if I miss it I shall catch the 8.47'. The second sentence implies a state of simple uncertainty. We could rephrase them in the 'If not . . . then . . .' form, thus: 'If I don't catch the 8.23 I shall catch the 8.47' and 'If it isn't the 7th today then it's the 8th'.

But these sentences seem to weight what originally appeared to be an equally balanced alternative in favour of the first one named. ('I intend to catch the 8.23 but if I don't . . .'. 'I *think* it's the 7th, but if it isn't . . .'.) So that although the simple alternative can be expressed in the 'If . . . then . . .' form the emphasis is usually altered by doing so and the link which is expressed by 'then' is of a rather different kind.

To sum up: if we examine all the cases we can find of 'either . . . or . . .' in which we are acquainted with the terms we shall find very few where we can add 'or both'. The object of expressing the thought in this way is often to emphasize the exclusion of both, to point out that it is not possible to have it both ways. If we are using the phrase ourselves therefore and want to mean 'or both' we are more likely to communicate our meaning effectively if we either use the 'If . . . then . . .' form or add 'or both'. It is interesting also to notice that 'either' placed at the very beginning of the sentence often seems to emphasize that the alternative is exclusive.

The 'If . . . then . . .' form, however, is very often used when the condition is only sufficient and not necessary. It is wise, therefore, to interpret it as excluding necessary unless we have reason to know otherwise from our acquaintance with the terms involved. And if we want to express the fact that p states a sufficient *and* necessary condition for q we shall do well to say so by adding, for example, 'and vice versa'.

Very often, however, we do not want to specify whether the condition is also necessary, this may be either because we don't know or because it is not relevant to the argument we are pursuing.

'NOT BOTH ... AND ...'

Proposition (1) on p. 70 could also be expressed in the form: 'It is not possible for a triangle both to have its sides in the ratio 3 : 4 : 5 and not to be right-angled.'

In general if q necessarily follows from p then it is not possible both to have p and $\bar{q}$.

'If p, then q' is clearly equivalent to 'If p, then not $\bar{q}$' or to '*Not both p and $\bar{q}$*'.

This is called the *disjunctive* form of the sentence 'If p, then q' and calls for no particular comment.

It is of some slight logical interest but in fact we do not often use it.

'ONLY IF ...'

A slightly puzzling but very useful phrase which does not seem to be quite consistently used is 'only if . . .'. It is used generally to imply that the condition is necessary but not sufficient.

We might say, for example: 'Only if a triangle is right-angled has it got sides in the ratio 3 : 4 : 5.' This would be used to mean:

'Only those triangles that are right-angled, but *not all of them*, have sides in the ratio 3 : 4 : 5.'

It would certainly not be true to say: 'Only if a triangle has sides in the ratio 3 : 4 : 5 is it right-angled.'

A useful way of communicating the fact that the condition is both sufficient and necessary is to say: 'If and only if . . .' as in the sentence: 'If and only if a quadrilateral is a parallelogram are both pairs of opposite sides equal.'

The phrase 'only if' does sometimes seem to be used by itself, however, to imply the same as 'if and only if . . .'. If a chess-player says: 'Only if you move your king there will you avoid being mated next move' he must mean that the condition is sufficient as well as necessary.

In fact when we use the phrase, as we often do, to refer to future events or intentions we sometimes insert a qualifying 'may' or 'might' to show that the condition is not sufficient but only necessary.

For example: 'Only if it stops raining might I go for a walk this afternoon.' (An essential condition for my even considering going for a walk is that it should stop raining: but it isn't certain that I shall go even if it does); or: 'Only if they can score at 90 runs an hour are they likely to think of declaring at lunch-time.'

S a P (see Ch. 3, p.35).

It will not have escaped the reader's attention that many of the sentences which we have examined in a hypothetical form could also have been put in the *S a P* form.

When we say, for example, 'If the sides of a triangle are in the ratio of 3 : 4 : 5 then it is right-angled' we could equally well say 'All triangles whose sides are in the ratio of 3 : 4 : 5 are right-angled'. In the first case the form of the sentence leaves open the question whether the condition is necessary as well as sufficient, and in the second case it is left open whether the situation is to be represented by Euler's circles thus

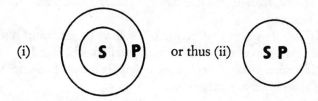

(i)   **S** **P**   or thus (ii)   **S P**

The state of affairs where the condition is sufficient but not necessary corresponds to diagram (i) and where it is both sufficient *and* necessary to diagram (ii).

In fact from our knowledge of Geometry we know that diagram (i) represents the true state of affairs.

Here there is very little to choose between the *S a P* method and the hypothetical method of expressing the geometrical fact, but most of the other hypothetical sentences we have been considering in this chapter would appear strangely artificial and distorted if put in the *S a P* form and would be likely to do their job of communicating less effectively.

If the sentence 'If *p*, then *q*', is taken to represent an example where the condition is sufficient but not necessary we have seen that the following sentences are equivalent to it:

(i) 'If *q̄*, then *p̄*'
(ii) Either *p̄*, or *q* (or both)
(iii) Not both *p* and *q̄*.

And sometimes there is a sentence of the form *S a P* which, without artificiality, can be said to be equivalent too.

'BECAUSE ... THEREFORE ...'

We have so far mostly used 'If . . . then . . .' as the words connecting the two linked propositions.

'Because . . . therefore . . .' is another way of expressing the fact that there is a logical or causal link, but it is used of the present or past and not of the future, and it is used more often for particular cases than for the statement of general principles.

For example:

(i) 'If you let go of that pen it will fall to the ground,' but 'Because you let go of that pen therefore it fell to the ground.'

(ii) 'If a man is cruel he causes unhappiness,' but 'Because James is cruel he causes unhappiness.'

All that has been said about necessary and sufficient conditions, the logical structure of 'If p then q' and the statements which are equivalent to it apply similarly to 'Because p, therefore q'.

THE 'LINK'

Although it has not always been material to our argument whether the propositions we have been considering were true or false it has almost always been obvious whether they were or not. We have been able to decide this from our experience and our knowledge of the terms involved.

It will be worth examining now rather more closely the nature of the link which connects p and q when we say 'If p, then q', or 'Because p, therefore q'.

We saw in the last chapter that the link could be deductive, that is a 'drawing out' of what is contained in the original proposition together with other propositions and axioms assumed to be known: all purely mathematical arguments are of this type. It can also be inductive, that is derived from experience: most scientific arguments are basically of this type.

It can be a description of past cause and effect or a forecast of future cause and effect. It can be the expression of an intention. It can be the explanation of the meaning of a word.

But all arguments, however complicated, can be analysed and broken up into a series of propositions of the form 'If p, then q' *or* 'Because p, therefore q'. In order to test the strength, therefore, of the reasoning of other people and to produce valid reasoning of our own we must pay careful attention to the nature and the validity of each of the links in the chain.

We shall now examine and analyse some examples.

(1) 'If a man is an Anarchist then he is a rogue. But Fotheringay is a rogue, therefore he is an Anarchist.'

This is clearly an example of the illegitimate inference of 'If q, then p' from 'If p, then q'. Being an Anarchist is stated to be a sufficient but not a necessary condition for being a rogue. Or, to put it in another way, although it is stated that all Anarchists are rogues it is not stated that all rogues are Anarchists.

(2) 'If my son is idle he will fail in his examination; if he over-works he will be ill. But either he will be idle or he will overwork. Therefore he will either fail in his examination or be ill.'

(Susan Stebbing: *A Modern Elementary Logic, p.* 51.)

This is of the form:

> If p, then q
> if r, then s;
> but either p or r
> ∴ either q or s.

It is easy to see that there is nothing wrong with the form of the argument. If we accept the 3 propositions: 'If p, then q', 'If r, then s', 'either p or r', then the conclusion certainly follows. But it is also easy to see that although the first two would probably be accepted—(but it does depend on *how* idle and on *how hard* he overworks)—there is no reason why the third one should be. Most of us in fact aim to steer a middle course between being idle and overworking and to say that one must be either the one or the other might be described as a false dilemma.

(3) 'If the sprockets are barboniferous, then the wingles cannot

be level; either the wingles must be level or the spums will be upset; you cannot hope to combine upset spums with a stable currency; but the sprockets are barboniferous, therefore the currency will not be stable.'

Let us represent the propositions by the letters p, q, r, s in the order of their occurrence.

Then, the argument runs:

'If p, then $\bar{q}$; either q or r; not both r and s; but p, therefore $\bar{s}$.' Or, if we arrange all the propositions in the form 'If . . . then . . .' it becomes:

> 'If p, then $\bar{q}$
> If $\bar{q}$, then r
> If r, then $\bar{s}$
> But p, $\therefore$ $\bar{s}$.'

And the argument is clearly seen to be valid.

(4) 'Only selfish people drive dangerously and few selfish people are teetotal. So most dangerous drivers drink.'

We will start by considering the logical form of this argument, supposing that we don't know what it is to be selfish, drive dangerously or be teetotal. We therefore put the argument in this form:

> 'Only A's are B's
> Few A's are C's
> $\therefore$ most B's are not C's'

where A's, B's, C's stand for selfish people, dangerous drivers and teetotallers respectively. The facts might be represented thus:

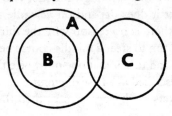

or thus:

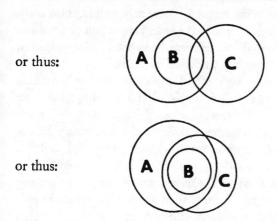

or thus:

Each of these arrangements is in accordance with the premisses but it will be seen that in one case no dangerous drivers are teetotallers, in another some of them are, and in the third all of them are. It is not therefore possible from the 'logical' form of the argument to come to any conclusion as to whether dangerous drivers drink. But it cannot be emphasized too strongly that to represent the argument thus is not a logical but a highly illogical thing to do. The classes of selfish people and dangerous drivers are certainly not clear-cut ones, though the class of teetotallers, if taken literally, is. All of us are selfish sometimes about certain things, and few people who drive cars can claim never to have driven dangerously, although it is certainly true that some people do it more often than others. The thought which lies behind 'only selfish people drive dangerously' would be expressed in a less misleading way by saying: 'To drive dangerously is a selfish thing to do' (and one might go on to add that many people who are selfish in this way are found to be selfish in other ways too).

To say that few selfish people are teetotal assumes again that there is a clearly defined class of selfish people: the thought behind the sentence would seem to be a general association of selfishness with not being teetotal. There may well be some truth in the conclusion in the sense that a large proportion of accidents may be attributable to drink: this may be verified by investigation but it cannot be 'proved' by analytical methods.

Euler's circles can be very useful, as we have seen, when one is reasoning about classes which are clear-cut or nearly so, but their use can, as in this example, be exceedingly misleading. We must be able to recognize whether a thought can reasonably be expressed in terms of a proposition of classes; to attempt to do so for thoughts of the type 'it is foolish to sit in a draught' is an abuse of logic. We must try the whole time to keep our thinking flexible and supple and ensure that the logical rules, Euler's circles, the forms of grammar and of inference are our servants and not our masters.

CERTAINTY

The propositions which we have been considering in this chapter have on the whole been of a kind where we could assert unequivocally whether they were true or false. When we said 'If p, then q' was true we meant that it was necessarily always true, and if this were not so, if the situation was really 'If p, then perhaps q' the proposition was considered to be false.

But in fact a great deal of our reasoning and argument is concerned not with certainties but with possibilities or probabilities. We say that if it is a fine day tomorrow we shall probably go on an expedition; the sky is red tonight so it looks like being fine; therefore it is quite likely that we shall go.

There are two uncertain links here—the first that *if* it is fine we shall *probably* go, the second that it *'looks like being'* (or will *probably* be) fine. The certainty of the conclusion is therefore clearly less than that of either of the links. It is worth noticing too that the uncertainties are of slightly different kinds. The first implies that whoever is in charge of the party has not yet made up his mind; it may be because there are other events which might happen tomorrow—Cousin Harriet and her family coming over to see us—which could affect the issue, or it may be just because he is not the sort of person who makes up his mind much in advance. The second uncertainty is about the way in which the weather will behave. Different people who fancy their skill as meteorologists will hold opinions about the weather to varying degrees of psychological certainty. Whether in fact it is now 'decided' what the weather will do tomorrow is a difficult metaphysical question, the important thing is that we cannot feel completely certain about it, though we may feel fairly confident.

It is much nicer and simpler to be able to deal with certainties, and that of course is why the deductive fields, (such as pure mathematics) where we get the complete certainty which we have put into our axioms or definitions, have formed the basis for the building up of logic.

But in real life we have uncertainties and it is important that our methods of thinking about them should be as valid and as accurate as possible.

It is clear that the same rules apply to 'probable' propositions as to 'certain' ones.

'If p then probably q' is equivalent to 'If $\bar{q}$, then probably $\bar{p}$', and similarly the other equivalent sentences will have to be qualified by probably, or by 'I think'.

Similarly again we cannot validly infer from 'If p, then probably q', 'If q then probably p.'

It would be true to say, for example, 'If he is an Australian he is probably keen on cricket,' but it would not be true to say: 'If he is keen on cricket then he is probably an Australian.' Quite often when 'If p, then probably q' is true, 'If q, then probably p' is also true, but not necessarily.

Obviously in a chain of argument in which there are many separate uncertainties the conclusion is more uncertain than any of them. It would not be true to say here that the chain is as weak as the weakest link, it is a good deal weaker.

Here is an example of a chain of logical argument with uncertain links: 'The twin problems with which the Chancellor is confronted today are the external balance of payments and the internal inflationary situation. The credit squeeze is designed to cure both. Bankers as a whole are likely to accede to his request to cut down credit, and if they do so the result should be a smaller effective purchasing power in the hands of the consuming public. Total demand is therefore curtailed and it is to be hoped that in particular there will be a slackening in demand both for goods that are suitable for export and for those that are at present being imported. This should have the double effect of increasing our exports and diminishing our imports. The certainty and effectiveness of this chain of events will obviously be reinforced by the effect of the credit squeeze on the internal level of prices. Our exports will undoubtedly cost less and will therefore be more attractive to foreigners to buy and the fact that our home-produced goods will now be cheaper than their foreign counter-parts provides an additional reason for a lessening of demand for imports.'

This argument, which is a typical piece of economic thinking, is seen to consist largely of links such as 'If *p* then *probably* (or some equivalent phrase) *q*'. It is inevitable that this should be so: the science of economics like most things in real life is compounded of uncertainties, but it is none the less useful material for us to use to exercise our logical faculties. We can estimate the validity of the chain and we can come to some conclusion, from our knowledge and experience of the terms involved and perhaps by experiment and the examination of Statistics, about the strength of the probabilities and how securely grounded are such phrases as 'it is to be hoped'.

It is worth noticing also in this passage an example of a dishonest ruse which is sometimes, regrettably, used in political and other arguments.

Where the chain consists of many uncertain links the speaker or writer will go out of his way to emphasize, even to over-emphasize, the uncertainty of some of the stronger links. By doing so he aims at giving the impression of being an eminently reasonable, fair-minded person who is very anxious not to claim too much. In this way he lulls his audience into a trusting, un-critical state. When he comes to what is in reality an exceedingly weak link in his argument, a proposition which is highly un-certain, he asserts it with a confidence ('undoubtedly', 'obvious-ly') which is quite unwarranted. But if his previous tactics have been successful in building up confidence he has a good chance of getting away with it.

SYMBOLIC LOGIC

We shall now describe and explain a particular example of a closed system of thinking. It is not at all essential to the main scheme of the book and in the reading of subsequent chapters it will be no handicap to have omitted it. Those readers who are mathematically minded and find the handling of symbols easy will no doubt take it in their stride, at the same time we would urge those who tend to be put off by symbols to attempt to understand it; once a few simple ideas have been grasped the theory and practice of what follows is not at all difficult although the symbols may appear alarming at first sight.

The system is a closed one, and as such it is inevitably arti-ficial. It deals with propositions which are assumed to be such that they must be either true or false. In other words the Logic is two-valued only; as we have seen, for a great many proposi-tions there are many intermediate shades of grey between the black and white of falsehood and truth.

But with this assumption—that a proposition must be either

G

true or false—there are, for two propositions p and q together, four possibilities; p and q both true; p true, q false; p false, q true; p and q both false.

These possibilities can be represented in a table thus:

p	q
T	T
T	F
F	T
F	F

where T stands for true and F for false. The truth or falsehood of a proposition is called its *value*, and tables setting out the value of simple and compound propositions are called *value tables*, or *truth tables*.

TRUTH TABLES

Consider the compound proposition 'p or q or both'. This proposition is clearly only false if p and q are both false, otherwise it is true. The 'values' (truth or falsehood) of this new proposition, which we shall call 'r', may be set out as follows:

p	q	r
T	T	T
T	F	T
F	T	T
F	F	F

The symbol which will be used for the proposition r is $p \vee q$, and although we used words above to describe and explain the origin of this proposition, its *definition* is contained in the table. It is a proposition which is false if and only if *p* and *q* are both false.

The definitions of, and the symbols for, other compound propositions may similarly be set out in a table thus:

p	*q*	*r*	*s*	*t*	*u*	*w*
T	T	T	T	F	T	T
T	F	T	F	T	F	F
F	T	T	F	T	F	T
F	F	F	F	F	T	T
		$p \vee q$	$p \cdot q$	p/q	$p \equiv q$	$p \supset q$

s is defined as a proposition which is true if *p* and *q* are both true but false otherwise. It is natural to call this the proposition '*p* and *q*': it is usually denoted by the symbol '*p . q*'.

t is defined as a proposition which is true if one and only one of the propositions *p* and *q* are true: it is natural to describe this as '*p* or *q*, but not both'. It is denoted by '*p/q*'.

u is defined as a proposition which is true if *p* and *q* have the same values and false if they have different values. It is natural to describe this by saying '*p* is equivalent to *q*'. It is denoted by '*p ≡ q*'.

w is defined as a proposition which is false if and only if *p* is true and *q* is false. Its verbal description as '*p* implies, or entails *q*' may not be so obviously apt as the other descriptions. It is denoted by '*p ⊃ q*'.

It must be emphasized again that the *meaning* of '*p ⊃ q*', and the other symbols, is *defined* by the value table. To discuss, when one has been introduced to these propositions, whether if *p* implies *q* it is the case that if *p* is false *q* may be either true or false, and therefore to wonder whether the table is right, would not be sensible and would show a misunderstanding of the situation. But '$p \supset q$' having been defined as it is in the table it would be perfectly sensible to discuss whether 'p implies, or entails q' are satisfactory ways of describing this relationship in words.

CONTRADICTORY

We have already met the contradictory of p or the denial or negation of p. We have used the symbol '$\bar{p}$' to denote it, but it is sometimes more convenient, for example when double negatives are involved, to use the symbol '$\sim p$'. The formal definition of $\bar{p}$ or $\sim p$ is contained in this table:

p	$\sim p$
T	F
F	T

MORE COMPLICATED PROPOSITIONS

Suppose now that we want to investigate the values of the compound propositions '$\bar{p} \lor q$' and '$\bar{q} \supset \bar{p}$', i.e. we want to discover whether they are true or false for the various combinations of truth and falsehood of p and q.

The values of $p, q, \bar{p}, \bar{q}$ can be set down thus:

p	q	$\bar{p}$	$\bar{q}$	$\bar{p}$ v q	$\bar{q}$ ⊃ $\bar{p}$
T	T	F	F		
T	F	F	T		
F	T	T	F		
F	F	T	T		

In order to fill up the column under '$\bar{p} \lor q$' we look at the value of $\bar{p}$ and q, in that order, and we refer to the definition of '$\lor$' in the basic table on p. 89. This shows us that the compound proposition '∨' is false only if the constituent propositions are both false: otherwise it is true. $\bar{p}$ and q are only both false in the second row, and it is therefore only in this row that the proposition '$\bar{p} \vee q$' has the value F. Again, reference to the basic table shows us that the compound proposition ' ⊃ ' is false only if the first of the two constituent propositions is true and the second false. As the two constituent propositions are $\bar{q}$ and $\bar{p}$, in that order, we see that it is only in the second row that the proposition '$\bar{q} \supset \bar{p}$' is false. The columns can therefore be filled up thus:

p	q	$\bar{p}$	$\bar{q}$	$\bar{p} \vee q$	$\bar{q} \supset \bar{p}$
T	T	F	F	T	T
T	F	F	T	F	F
F	T	T	F	T	T
F	F	T	T	T	T

The two compound propositions '$\bar{p} \vee q$' and '$\bar{q} \supset \bar{p}$' are seen to have the same values and they are therefore called equivalent. This fact could also be stated symbolically thus: $(\bar{p} \vee q) \equiv (\bar{q} \supset \bar{p})$. (We have seen that '$p \supset q$' is best represented verbally by 'p implies q' which is for most purposes the same as 'if p then q'. '$\bar{q} \supset \bar{p}$' therefore becomes 'if $\bar{q}$ then $\bar{p}$' which as we saw on p. 72 is equivalent to 'if p then q'.

Again '$\bar{p} \vee q$' can be represented verbally by 'not-p or q or both' and we saw on p. 73 that this is logically equivalent to 'if p, then q'. The fact that these compound propositions are equivalent could therefore have been deduced without the assistance of truth tables.)

We will now set out the Truth Table for a compound proposition of greater complexity. Consider the following:

$$\{[\sim(p/q)] \vee (p \cdot \bar{q})\} \supset \{(q \cdot p)/(\bar{p} \vee q)\}.$$

Notice that the brackets, as in simple arithmetic and algebra, indicate the order in which the operations are to be carried out or the values discovered. Here the main symbol whose values will have to be discovered last is clearly $\supset$. This is the table for the above proposition:

					(1)	(2)	(3)	(4)	(5)	(6)	(7)
p	q	$\bar{p}$	$\bar{q}$	p/q	$\{[\sim(p/q)]$	$\lor$	$(p\cdot\bar{q})\}$	$\supset$	$\{(q\cdot p)$	$/$	$(\bar{p}\lor q)\}$
T	T	F	F	F	T	T	F	F	T	F	T
T	F	F	T	T	F	T	F	F	F	T	F
F	T	T	F	T	F	T	T	T	F	T	T
F	F	T	T	T	T	F	F	T	F	T	T

After filling up the columns $p, q, \bar{p}, \bar{q}$ fill up p/q. Column (1) is then the negation of this. Next fill up column (3) by considering the values of p and $\bar{q}$ in accordance with the definition of $\cdot\cdot$ Then fill up column (2) by considering the values of (1) and (3) in accordance with the definition of $\lor$. This column gives us the values of the proposition $\{[\sim(p/q)] \lor (p\cdot\bar{q})\}$.

We now fill up the columns (5) and (7) and then, by considering the conjunction of their values with the symbol $/$, column (6). Column (4), which is '(2) $\supset$ (6)', can now be filled up to give us the final values of the whole proposition. These are seen to be F, F, T, T.

If the truth values of a compound proposition are all T the proposition is said to be a *Tautology*. (It is also sometimes said to be analytic.) If, as in the proposition we have just been investigating, the values are a mixture of T and F the proposition is said to be *contingent*. If the values are all F, the proposition is said to be *self-contradictory*.

There is no reason of course why a compound proposition should not incorporate three or more simple propositions p, q, r etc. If this is so the truth tables will be more complicated but the principle will be exactly the same.

Consider, for example, the proposition:

$$\{(p|\bar{r}) \supset (r \vee \bar{q})\} \cdot (q \supset \bar{p}).$$

In order to find the values of this we must first set down all the possible combinations of values of p, q and r. As we saw above, four rows are required for all the possible combinations for p and q; since for each of these combinations r can have the value T or F eight rows will be required altogether. It will be simpler and clearer if we then set out the values of $\bar{p}$, $\bar{q}$ and $\bar{r}$. The rest of the table can then be filled up.

						(1)	(2)	(3)	(4)	(5)
p	q	r	$\bar{p}$	$\bar{q}$	$\bar{r}$	$\{p|\bar{r}$	$\supset$	$(r \vee \bar{q})\}$	$\cdot$	$q \supset \bar{p}$
T	T	T	F	F	F	T	T	T	F	F
T	T	F	F	F	T	F	T	F	F	F
T	F	T	F	T	F	T	T	T	T	T
T	F	F	F	T	T	F	T	T	T	T
F	T	T	T	F	F	F	T	T	T	T
F	T	F	T	F	T	T	F	F	F	T
F	F	T	T	T	F	F	T	T	T	T
F	F	F	T	T	T	T	T	T	T	T

Columns (1), (3) and (5) must be filled up first. Column (2) is then obtained by combining (1) and (3) in accordance with the definition of $\supset$. Column (4) which gives the values of the whole proposition is then obtained by combining (2) and (5) in accordance with the definition of $\cdot$. It will be seen that the proposition is contingent.

Examples on Chapter 5

1. Arrange the following 16 sentences in equivalent groups:
    (i) If q, then p.
    (ii) Either p or $\bar{q}$, or both.
    (iii) If $\bar{p}$ then q.
    (iv) Not both p and $\bar{q}$.
    (v) Either $\bar{p}$ or $\bar{q}$ or both.
    (vi) If p then $\bar{q}$.
    (vii) If $\bar{q}$ then $\bar{p}$.
    (viii) Not both $\bar{p}$ and q.
    (ix) Either p or q or both.
    (x) If q, then $\bar{p}$.
    (xi) Not both $\bar{p}$ and $\bar{q}$.
    (xii) If p, then q.
    (xiii) Not both p and q.
    (xiv) If $\bar{q}$, then p.
    (xv) If $\bar{p}$ then $\bar{q}$.
    (xvi) Either $\bar{p}$ or q or both.

2. Examine and discuss the following argument: 'If we reject Pomeranians we have no alternative but to accept squeeches. Again if we will not take sea-water then river-water must be our lot. But there are no squeeches available, and we know that it follows from this that river-water is out of the question. It looks therefore as though we shall have to be content with Pomeranians or sea-water or both.'

3. Comment on the truth or otherwise of the following:

    (i) If p expresses a sufficient condition for q, it is not necessary for the condition to be necessary for the truth of q to be sufficiently established by that of p.

    (ii) If q expresses a necessary condition for p it is necessary also for the truth of p to be a necessary condition for the truth of q if the truth of q is to be sufficiently established by that of p.

    (iii) If p, q and r are each separately sufficient conditions for s, and s is also a sufficient condition for q, it must follow that not only must s and q be mutually necessary conditions for each other, but also that p and r must be mutually sufficient conditions for each other.

4. p and q are each necessary conditions for r; r is a sufficient condition for s; s and p are both sufficient conditions for x; x is a necessary condition for the falsehood of q. If q is known to be untrue what can you say about the truth or falsehood of p, r, s, x?

5. Either p or q is true or both; q and r cannot both be true; r is a sufficient condition and s a necessary condition for x; x is a necessary condition for p. If x is known to be false what can you say about p, q, r, s?

6. Two of the necessary qualifications for membership of the Eccentric Sportsmens Club are that one should have played Polo in Patagonia and Croquet in Czechoslovakia. In order to get a permit to play Croquet in Czechoslovakia one must be a founder member of the Hoop Club. One cannot be a founder member of the Hoop Club unless one has played Polo in Patagonia. Everybody must either be a member of the Eccentric Sportsmens Club or the Oddfellows Association or both, but one cannot both be a member of the Oddfellows Association and have played Croquet in Czechoslovakia.

What can you say about (i) Smith, who is not a founder member of the Hoop Club; (ii) Jones, who has played Croquet in Czechoslovakia; (iii) Robinson, who has not played Polo in Patagonia?

7. p and q are separately necessary and together sufficient conditions for r; r is a necessary condition for s; q and s cannot both be true and cannot both be false; x is true if and only if s is a sufficient condition for p; x is a sufficient condition for r. What can you say about the truth or falsehood of p, q, r, s, x?

8. Express the following sentences in (*a*) the alternative, (*b*) the disjunctive form. Say in each case which form you think is to be preferred.

    (i) If I can't find my hat I shall have to go without one.

    (ii) If we are to believe what the Captain says the ship is sinking fast.

    (iii) Unless you return the things which I have lent you I shall tell the Headmaster.

    (iv) If you take my Queen I shall be able to mate you next move.

    (v) If two angles are vertically opposite then they are equal.

    (vi) Only if a number is even is it divisible by 6.

(vii) If a quadrilateral is a square then its four angles are all right angles.

9. Express the following sentences in (*a*) the hypothetical, (*b*) the disjunctive form, and state in each case whether it would be proper to add 'or both'. State also which form you think is to be preferred.

(i) Either you get out of my garden at once or I shall call the police.

(ii) I will come to see you either on Monday or on Tuesday.

(iii) Either that figure is not a rectangle or its diagonals bisect one another.

(iv) Either you switch the petrol on or the car won't start.

(v) Either you take that butter out of the sun or it will melt.

10. Express the following sentences in (*a*) the hypothetical, (*b*) the alternative form. Say in each case which form you think is to be preferred.

(i) You can't expect to go on doing no work and then come top of the form.

(ii) It is not possible for a triangle to be right-angled and to have sides in the ratio 2 : 3 : 4.

(iii) You can't both have your cake and eat it.

(iv) You can't move your king there and avoid being mated next move.

(v) It is not possible for a triangle to have two sides equal and not to have two angles equal.

11. Smith is looking for his bicycle and his friends give him the following information:

(i) Either you don't look behind the coalshed or you won't find your bicycle.

(ii) If you don't fail to find your bicycle it's because you haven't looked under the dining-room table.

(iii) If you don't find your bicycle it's because you haven't looked in the front porch.

(iv) You can't both find your bicycle and not fail to look in the cycle shed.

Where should Smith look for his bicycle?

12. Arrange the following statements as far as possible into groups

which are equivalent to each other (assume that 'virtuous' and 'wicked' are contradictories).

    (i) If a man is virtuous then he is a Liberal.

    (ii) Either a man is a Liberal or he is not wicked or both.

    (iii) Only if a man is virtuous is he a Liberal.

    (iv) A man cannot both be wicked and not be a Liberal.

    (v) All Liberals are virtuous.

    (vi) If a man is not a Liberal then he is not wicked.

    (vii) Either a man is virtuous or he is not a Liberal or both.

    (viii) Only if a man is not a Liberal is he wicked.

13. You are told that all pomoxes are squameous and that some pomoxes are grifficorns. Which of the following remarks are true?

    (i) It is impossible not to be squameous without being a grifficorn.

    (ii) Either that is not a pomox or it is squameous.

    (iii) If that is neither squameous nor a grifficorn, then it cannot be a pomox.

14. In addition to the data of the last question, you are also told that all pomoxes always speak the truth, some grifficorns never do, and the rest always do. Did a pomox or a grifficorn make the following remarks, and are they true or false?

    (i) 'If I am a grifficorn then either I am not squameous or I must be a pomox. I wish I knew which I was!'

    (ii) 'I am a pomox and proud of it. I know I'm squameous but all my life I've set my face against Grifficornery. And after all some grifficorns are squameous too.'

15. Examine and discuss the following arguments:

    (i) It is a well-known fact that if a man is not a troglodyte then he is not frabjous, it is also commonly recognized that only if a man is not an Essentialist can he be suprapuntal. Clearly no one can be both a troglodyte and couth, and one must either be an Essentialist or frabjous or both. It therefore follows that since Jones is indubitably suprapuntal he cannot also be couth.

    (ii) All brave people have great strength of character. Most of those who are unable to give up smoking have weak characters. It therefore follows that most people who smoke are cowards.

(iii) To philosophize is to examine the basic problems of human existence with a clear unbiased mind; most sensible people therefore are philosophers at heart. Perhaps the most striking manifestation of good sense that we can find in the contemporary situation is the way in which more and more people are coming to appreciate the merits of the simple life. It is pleasant to be able to infer that simplicity is the essence of good philosophy.

16. Discuss the following argument and counter argument: An Athenian mother says to her son:

'If you say what is just, men will hate you; and if you say what is unjust the gods will hate you; but you must say what is just or what is unjust; hence either men will hate you or the gods will hate you.'

The son replies:

'If I say what is just the gods will love me; and if I say what is unjust, men will love me; but I must say one or the other; therefore either the gods will love me or men will love me.'

17. By constructing truth tables find out whether the following propositions are tautologous, contingent or self-contradictory:

(i) $p \supset (p \lor q)$

(ii) $(p/\bar{q}) \supset q$

(iii) $\{(p \lor q) \cdot \bar{p}\} \supset q$

(iv) $(\bar{p} \lor q) \equiv (\bar{q} \cdot p)$

(v) $\{\sim(p \cdot q)\} \equiv (\bar{p} \lor \bar{q})$

(vi) $\{\sim(p \supset \bar{q})\} / \{(\bar{p} \lor \bar{q}) \cdot p\}$

(vii) $\{q \supset (p \lor q)\} \supset \{(p \cdot q) \cdot (p/q)\}$

(viii) $\{(p \supset q) \cdot (p \supset r)\} \supset \{p \supset (q \cdot r)\}$

(ix) $\{(p \supset q) \cdot (q \cdot \bar{r})\} \supset \{(p \lor r) \cdot (\bar{r}/q)\}$.

18. On what days of the week, if any, are the following true?

(i) (Yesterday was Sunday) $\supset$ (Tomorrow is Tuesday).

(ii) (Today is Sunday) $\supset$ (Today is Saturday).

(iii) (Tomorrow is not Sunday) $\supset$ (Yesterday was Friday).

(iv) (Yesterday was Sunday)/(Tomorrow is Wednesday).

(v) (Tomorrow is Thursday) . (Yesterday was not Tuesday).

(vi) (Tomorrow is not Monday) $\lor$ (Today is Thursday).

19. At what times of the day, if any, are the following true?

(i) (It's not yet 7.0 p.m.) $\supset$ (It's after 5.0 p.m.)

(ii) (It's between 7.0 a.m. and 9.0 a.m.)/(It's between 8.0 a.m. and 10.0 a.m.)

(iii) (It's after 6.0 p.m.) ≡ [(It's not yet 5.0 p.m.) ⊃ (It's before noon)].

20. Who could truthfully make the following statements when?

(i) [(I'm John Jones) ∨ (It's March 4th)] . [(It's May 10th)/(I'm Sidney Smith)]

(ii) ∼[(p . q) ⊃ {∼(r/s)}]

where p stands for 'I'm Caesar'

where q stands for 'It's between 6 and 8 p.m.'

where r stands for 'It's between 7 and 9 p.m.'

where s stands for 'I'm Cleopatra'.

21. On being questioned about his age a man replies:

$$(p/q) . [\sim(r \supset s)]$$

If p stands for 'I'm over 70'

If q stands for 'I'm not between 45 and 55'

If r stands for 'I'm between 40 and 50'

If s stands for 'I'm under 35',

what conclusion can you come to about how old he says he is?

22. If p stands for 'I had bacon for breakfast'

If q stands for 'I had kippers for breakfast'

If r stands for 'I had sausages for breakfast',

and if the statement

$$\{(p . \bar{q}) \vee (q \supset r)\}/\{[\bar{r} \vee (q . \bar{p})] \supset (r . \bar{p})\}$$

is true, what can you say about what I had for breakfast?

23. Express $p . q$ by using only the symbols ∼ and ⊃ .

24. Express $p . q$ by using only the symbols ∼ and ∨.

25. Express ∼($p ∨ \bar{q}$) by using only the symbols ∼ and . .

6

The Syllogism

A particular form of argument to which great importance used
to be attached runs as follows:

> All Frenchmen are Europeans;
> Henri is a Frenchman;
> ∴ Henri is a European.

It will be seen that it consists of two statements or premisses from
the combination of which it is claimed that the third line, the
conclusion, follows. It is easy to see that in the example we have
selected the conclusion is true provided that the premisses are
true.

This is an example of what is called a 'syllogism'.

It used to be claimed that all argument and all our reasoning
could be reduced to a series of syllogisms. It is now agreed that
although many arguments can be put into a syllogistic form this
is often only possible by an unnatural twisting and warping of
our thinking, and it is not a particularly useful thing to do.

No study of Logic, however, would be complete without some
mention of the syllogism and we propose in this chapter, without
going into too much detail, to give some brief outline of the forms
which the syllogism can take and to examine the sort of arguments which appear naturally in the syllogistic shape.

PREMISSES AND TERMS

The two premisses of a syllogism are called the *Major* and
Minor premisses respectively. Each premiss is expressed in one of
Aristotle's four propositional forms which we considered in

Chapter 3. Each premiss therefore has a Subject, Copula and Predicate, and either asserts that 'All . . . are . . .', that 'Some . . . are . . .', that 'No . . . are . . .' or that 'Some . . . are not . . .'.

The shorthand ways of writing these are, it will be remembered, $S\,a\,P,\ S\,i\,P,\ S\,e\,P,\ S\,o\,P$. (It will also be remembered that a singular proposition such as: 'Henri is a Frenchman' counts as a universal proposition; reference is made to *all* the members of the class, but there is only one.)

Clearly if a conclusion is to follow from the union of the two premisses they must have something in common. If after saying that all Frenchmen are Europeans I then go on to say that Henri is a Swiss, there is no conclusion that can be drawn from these two statements; they are entirely independent of each other. The item or *term* (in this case *Frenchmen*) which comes in both Premisses is called the *Middle term*. The other term which comes in the first or Major premiss is called the Major term (*European* in the example quoted) and the other term in the Minor premiss is called the Minor term (in this case *Henri*). It is conventional that the Minor term is the subject of the conclusion, and the Major term its predicate. We shall denote the Major, Middle and Minor terms by $P,\ M,\ S$ respectively.

Clearly the Middle term which mediates between or connects the other two will not itself appear in the conclusion but the Major and Minor terms both will.

THE FIGURES OF A SYLLOGISM

Here are some more examples of syllogisms:
   (1) No birds are four-legged;
       All sparrows are birds;
       ∴ no sparrows are four-legged.
   (2) All judges are lawyers;
       No bishops are lawyers;
       ∴ no bishops are judges.

(3) All schoolmasters are serious;
    Some schoolmasters are good-looking;
    ∴ some good-looking people are serious.

(4) No Communists are members of my club;
    Some members of my club are Old Etonians;
    ∴ some Old Etonians are not Communists.

These syllogisms are all obviously valid.

From what has been said about P, M, S it will be seen that the structure of these four syllogisms can be exhibited as follows:

$$
\begin{array}{llll}
(1)\ \ M-P & (2)\ \ P-M & (3)\ \ M-P & (4)\ \ P-M \\
\quad\ \ S-M & \quad\ \ S-M & \quad\ \ M-S & \quad\ \ M-S \\
\hline
\therefore\ S-P & \therefore\ S-P & \therefore\ S-P & \therefore\ S-P
\end{array}
$$

The important difference between these 4 arrangements is the position of M: it will be seen that they exhaust the possibilities. Either M is the subject of the major premiss and the predicate of the minor (as in (1)), or it is the predicate in both (as in (2)), or it is the subject in both (as in (3)), or it is the predicate of the major premiss and the subject of the minor.

These differences are said to be differences in the *figure* of a syllogism, so that a syllogism can be in any one of the four figures above.

(It will not be of great importance for our purposes which number is attached to which arrangement. But the conventional numbering is as above and it may help the reader to remember this if he notices that a line drawn through the M's when the four figures are put consecutively side by side as above produces a rough W thus \|\|/.)

It should now be clear that with a given set of terms a great many different syllogisms will be possible, some of which will be valid and some not. In the first figure, for example, the major premiss can be in any one of the four forms $M\,a\,P$, $M\,i\,P$, $M\,e\,P$, $M\,o\,P$; and with each of these the minor premiss can be in any one of the forms $S\,a\,M, S\,i\,M, S\,e\,M, S\,o\,M$. This gives altogether 16 possible arrangements of the two premisses.

With each of these arrangements it is theoretically possible to have any one of the 4 forms $S\,a\,P, S\,i\,P, S\,e\,P, S\,o\,P$, in the conclusion. This gives altogether 64 (i.e. 16 × 4) syllogisms in the first figure and therefore 4 times 64 or 256 syllogisms altogether. As a matter of interest only 19 of these are valid.

VALIDITY CONSIDERED

In a more systematic treatment of the syllogism various axioms and rules would be given whereby the validity of different examples could be determined. We shall content ourselves here with deriving one or two of these rules by inspection and common sense and deciding similarly whether various arrangements yield a valid syllogism.

Consider for example:

    (1) Some books are detective stories;
        Some books are novels;
          ∴ some novels are detective stories;

and

    (2) Some books are mathematical text-books;
        Some books are novels;
          ∴ some novels are mathematical text-books.

In both examples both premisses are clearly true.

In the first example the conclusion is also true, but in the second it is false. But the two syllogisms are both of exactly the same pattern, namely:

$$M\,i\,P$$
$$\underline{M\,i\,S}$$
$$\therefore S\,i\,P$$

Is this pattern valid?

Obviously not. For a syllogism to be valid it must always pro-

H

duce a true conclusion from true premisses and this one does not do so. It is easy to see why and to derive from that reason a general principle. The middle term in both syllogisms is 'some books'. But there is no reason why the 'some books' of the major premiss should include any of the 'some books' of the minor premiss. This middle term, in fact, although it consists of the same two words may refer to two completely different sets of objects which have nothing in common at all. In such a case therefore it cannot do its job of 'mediating' between the other two and no conclusion can be claimed to follow: it is as though there were four different terms instead of three. This criticism obviously applies whenever the middle term refers only to 'some' of a class on both occasions on which it is used (or in technical phraseology when the middle term is *undistributed*).

All such syllogisms would therefore be invalid.

But it is perfectly possible to have a valid syllogism with the middle term prefaced by 'some' in one of its appearances provided that it is prefaced by 'All' or 'No' in the other one.

For example:

None of the inhabitants of Rutland are friends of Numbskull;

Some of the inhabitants of Rutland are friends of Golightly;

∴ Some of Golightly's friends are not friends of Numbskull.

This is clearly a valid syllogism.

The reader will find at the end of the chapter examples which will give him the opportunity of testing for himself his ability to see by inspection whether various syllogisms are valid or not.

Although we do not often find ordinary arguments in the precise syllogistic shape there are many more or less disguised syllogisms, arguments which quite easily can be put in that shape, and which will often be easier to examine and to test for validity if they are.

Consider for example:

(1) 'If a man is a Conservative he cannot also advocate a

deliberately unbalanced Budget. It follows therefore that
no Conservatives believe in Nationalization, for all those
who support the calculated failure to balance our National
Accounts are firm supporters also of Nationalization.'

In order to express this argument in the form of a syllogism
and then analyse it, it will be easiest to start by finding the conclusion. The words 'it follows therefore' form our signpost to the
fact that 'No Conservatives believe in Nationalization' is the
conclusion. 'Believers in Nationalization' must therefore be our
major term, and 'Conservatives' our minor. 'Advocates of a
deliberately unbalanced Budget' is then seen to be the middle
term. The syllogism therefore runs like this:

'All advocates of a deliberately unbalanced Budget are believers in Nationalization;

No Conservatives are advocates of a deliberately unbalanced
Budget;

∴ No Conservatives are believers in Nationalization.'

This is the form

$$M \, a \, P$$
$$S \, e \, M$$
$$\therefore \overline{S \, e \, P}$$

Is it valid?

It should be obvious that it isn't. It only would be if the major
premiss implied that all the advocates of a deliberately unbalanced
Budget comprised *all* the believers in Nationalization, and there
is clearly no reason in fact or in logical form why this should be
so.

It is fallacious because from a premiss in which something is
said about *some* of the believers in Nationalization a conclusion is
drawn which purports to say something about *all* of them.

UNSTATED PREMISSES

A great many simple arguments of the form '*p*, ∴ *q*' might be
described as being syllogisms with one of the premisses left un-

stated, usually because it is so obvious as not to be worth mentioning.

If I say for example 'You won't be able to get in because you haven't got a ticket', I imply but don't actually say that 'only those who have tickets will be allowed in'.

In syllogistic form the argument, including the unstated premiss, might be put as follows:

'No persons other than ticket-holders are persons who will be allowed in;

You are a person other than a ticket-holder;

∴ You are a person who is not in the class of those allowed in.'

It may sometimes be useful that the unstated premiss should be formulated, for by doing that it may be easier to test the validity of the argument, but apart from this no particularly useful purpose is served by putting the argument in a syllogistic form.

We often use arguments, perhaps again with unstated premisses, which could be put in a syllogistic form but which do not claim to arrive at certain conclusions.

Suppose I say: 'I have some friends who are probably going to Spain for their summer holiday this year, so I expect they'll be pretty sunburnt in September.'

We could put this in what might be described as an 'uncertain' syllogistic form thus:

'People who are in Spain in the summer are likely to get sunburnt.

My friends are probably going to Spain for their summer holiday.

∴ My friends will probably be sunburnt in September.'

The major premiss here was originally unstated.

Again there is no particular merit in putting the argument like this, except that doing so may emphasize the fact that if both the premisses are uncertain the conclusion must be more uncertain than either of them.

Sometimes this uncertainty may be expressed more precisely.
We have seen that in general the syllogism

$$M \, i \, P$$
$$M \, i \, S$$
$$\therefore \overline{S \, i \, P}$$

is not valid because the Middle term is undistributed.

Let us consider again an actual example:

'Some Englishmen pay Income Tax;

Some Englishmen are in favour of a State Lottery;

∴ Some of those who pay Income Tax are in favour of a State Lottery.'

In general, as we have seen, this is not valid. But if we know that the 'some' of the major premiss comprises 65% of Englishmen, and the 'some' of the minor premiss 72% then we can see that there is bound to be an overlap and that we would be entitled to say that *some* of those who pay Income Tax are in favour of a State Lottery.

To be precise, out of every 100 Englishmen at least 37 must both pay Income Tax and be in favour of a State Lottery, and there might be as many as 65.

(The figure of 37 is arrived at as follows:

Out of 100 Englishmen 35 do not pay Income Tax and 28 are not in favour of State Lotteries. In order to get the *least* number who must be both Income Tax payers and in favour of State Lotteries we assume that there is no overlap between these groups of 35 and 28. We therefore add them together (63) and subtract from 100 to get the minimum number who are both payers of Income Tax and in favour of State Lotteries.)

Examples on Chapter 6
(In the following examples 'some' does not exclude 'all'.)

1. Do premisses in the following forms produce valid syllogisms? If so what are the conclusions? Justify your answer in each case and construct a verbal example.

(i) $P\ a\ M$
    $S\ e\ M$

(ii) $P\ i\ M$
    $M\ a\ S$

(iii) $M\ a\ P$
    $S\ o\ M$

(iv) $P\ e\ M$
    $S\ i\ M$

(v) $M\ e\ P$
    $M\ o\ S$

(vi) $P\ a\ M$
    $M\ e\ S$

2. Are the following syllogisms valid? If not explain why not. In each case put the premisses and conclusion in the $P\ a\ M$ etc. form.

(i) Some bald men are toothless;
Some Ethiopians are bald;
∴ some Ethiopians are toothless.

(ii) Some Frenchmen do not eat garlic;
All Frenchmen are Europeans;
∴ some Europeans eat garlic.

(iii) No chess-players are stupid;
Some stupid people play draughts;
∴ some draughts-players are not chess-players.

(iv) All clergymen believe in the abolition of capital punishment;
Some of those who believe in the abolition of capital punishment are Socialists;
∴ some Socialists are clergymen.

3. Put the following arguments in syllogistic form, supplying any premisses that are missing. State in each case whether the syllogism is a valid one. (You need not consider whether the premisses are true.)

(i) An increase in wages is always inflationary and therefore against the long-term interests of the workers.

(ii) If one travels 1st class with a 2nd class ticket one is likely to be prosecuted.

(iii) Since Jones is in favour of planning therefore he is a Communist.

4. Express the following arguments in syllogistic form if you think it possible to do so, and say whether they are valid. Discuss also the arguments as a whole including the soundness or otherwise of the premisses.

(i) Fashions in opinions as in everything else are continually changing. Opinions that are fashionable at any time often have a superficial appearance of subtlety about them. But to be subtle is not necessarily to be true. We need not hesitate to conclude, therefore, that some of the views which it is not fashionable to hold have about them the authentic stamp of truth.

(ii) It is pleasant to be able to record that at least some of our M.P.s may be described as right-minded people, for among those who were returned to Parliament at the last Election are to be found a substantial number who have expressed themselves in agreement with me.

(iii) It is a truism to say that all narrow-minded people are kill-joys. Since true broad-mindedness can only be attained by an Education that is both wide and deep it is on the teaching profession as a whole that our reputation for being a happy and joyful nation must rest.

5. Some Irishmen are Conservatives;
Some Irishmen play Rugby Football.
If the 'some' of the first line is 59% of all Irish males and the 'some' of the second line is 80% what can you say about how many of every 100 Irishmen are both Conservatives and Rugby Football players?

6. Which of the following statements are true of all valid Syllogisms? Justify your answers.

(i) At least one premiss must be affirmative.
(ii) The major premiss must be universal.
(iii) With one premiss negative, the conclusion must be negative.
(iv) The conclusion cannot be universal if the minor premiss is affirmative.
(v) If both premisses are negative the conclusion cannot be universal.
(vi) A term that is distributed in the conclusion must be distributed in the corresponding premiss.

(vii) If the major premiss is particular the minor premiss cannot be negative.

7. Which of the following statements are true of valid syllogisms of Figure 1? Justify your answers.

(i) The major premiss must be universal.

(ii) One premiss must be negative.

(iii) The minor premiss must be affirmative.

(iv) The conclusion must be particular.

8. Which of the following statements are true of valid syllogisms of Figure 2? Justify your answers.

(i) The conclusion cannot be universal if the minor premiss is affirmative.

(ii) Both premisses must be universal.

(iii) One premiss must be negative.

(iv) The major premiss must be universal.

9. Which of the following statements are true of valid syllogisms of Figure 3? Justify your answers.

(i) Neither premiss can be negative.

(ii) The conclusion must be particular.

(iii) The minor premiss must be affirmative.

(iv) The major premiss must be universal.

10. Which of the following statements are true of valid syllogisms of Figure 4? Justify your answers.

(i) The minor premiss must be affirmative.

(ii) The minor premiss cannot be particular if the major premiss is affirmative.

(iii) One premiss must be negative.

(iv) The major premiss cannot be particular if either premiss is negative.

(v) The conclusion cannot be universal if the minor premiss is affirmative.

11. Which syllogisms are valid in Figure 1?

12. Which syllogisms are valid in Figure 2?

13. Which syllogisms are valid in Figure 3?

14. Which syllogisms are valid in Figure 4?

7

Certainty and Probability

IN Chapter 4 (p. 56) reference was made to the difference between subjective and objective certainty and on several occasions degrees of certainty have been mentioned. We are now going to examine in more detail the whole concept of certainty, and the allied concept of probability; to consider just what it is to be certain and how the words 'certain' and 'probable' are used.

NECESSITY

We have seen already that if we take as our premisses axioms from a closed system of thinking, such as chess or mathematics, and apply processes of valid deductive reasoning to them, the conclusions which result have a certainty which seems to be of a different kind from that which can be claimed for the results of any inductive process of thought. If it is true that all A's are B's and that some A's are C's we know with certainty that it must follow that some B's are C's whatever kind of groups A, B, and C stand for. It might be said that this conclusion is objectively certain, but perhaps a better way to describe it would be to say that it follows *necessarily*, 'it is necessarily the fact that . . .' and this is so whatever any individuals may say about how certain they feel of the conclusion.

In what follows we shall use the word 'necessity' for what we have described as the objective certainty which results from valid deduction from axiomatic premisses. The use of a different word may help to emphasize more strongly the difference in kind between the two concepts for which the word 'certainty' preceded by the appropriate adjectives is used to stand.

When a statement or an argument about an open system, the world of our experience, is claimed to be necessarily true that claim can only be allowed if the necessity is derived from the definitions of the words or phrases which are being used.

The statement, for example, 'All Frenchmen are Europeans' is only necessarily true if the words 'Frenchmen' and 'Europeans' are used or defined in such a way as to make it true: if they were not so defined there could certainly be no necessity about it and it would always be possible that an exception might be found.

Again suppose that, as in a syllogism we used in the last chapter, we say: 'No Conservatives are advocates of a deliberately unbalanced Budget.' We could obviously only defend this as being necessarily true if we make part of our definition of a Conservative the characteristic of not advocating a deliberately unbalanced Budget, so that if someone were to claim, as otherwise he very likely might, that he had found a Conservative who did advocate a deliberately unbalanced Budget we should simply reply, 'Well in that case he can't be a Conservative, or at any rate not what *I* mean by a Conservative.'

The necessity of the statement or conclusion follows again, as with all necessary conclusions from deductive arguments in closed systems, from the fact that *we* put it there in the first place by the formulation of our axioms or the definition of our terms.

CERTAINTY

It has already been pointed out that we use the word 'certain' in two rather different ways. We may apply it to our own or to somebody else's state of mind ('I am certain that it rained yesterday') or we may apply it to outside things ('It is certain that William the Conqueror landed in 1066').

In both uses of the word we talk of degrees of certainty. In the first case we should use such phrases as 'I am fairly sure that . . .', 'I think that . . .', 'I am rather doubtful whether . . .'; and in the second case phrases such as 'it is probable, possible, unlikely that . . .'.

In the second use of the word 'it is certain that . . .' the certainty appears to be of an objective kind; we do not seem to be merely describing our own state of mind. But it is clearly not the same kind of objective certainty that we have agreed to call necessity, the kind which can be claimed for conclusions of some deductive arguments. 'Necessary' would obviously be an in appropriate adjective to apply to the statement about William the Conqueror.

And, as a matter of fact, *is* it quite certain? Might there not be some mistake about the date? Is it not possible that historical research might produce evidence for the theory that it was not William the Conqueror at all? Historians will no doubt say that this is exceedingly unlikely, as it obviously is, but one might just remark in passing that there have been a great many events for which certainty was claimed and on which considerable doubt has subsequently been thrown.

A more important point, however, is this. Exactly what do we mean when we say of a historical event that it is certain? A way of investigating what someone means when he says this would be by cross-examining him about the grounds for his statement, asking him in other words how he would verify it. He would no doubt say that it is a well-known fact, that he has read it in the history books, that expert historians have said so; and they have said it because they read it in books and it was thus handed down to them by the historians of a previous generation. And if one traces it far enough back one would almost certainly find that the first chronicler to record the event did so either because he had seen it himself or because he had got it from eye-witnesses.

It would seem therefore that an analysis of what one means

when one appears to claim objective certainty for a historical event reveals that one is really claiming that a great many people, many of them experts who have studied the evidence, now have, or have had in the past, a feeling of subjective or psychological certainty about it.

Phrases such as 'it is certain that . . .', 'it is a well-known fact that . . .', 'there is no doubt that . . .' are used frequently. They are sometimes used to invest a questionable statement with an air of authority when all that the speaker is really entitled to say is something like: 'A few people are certain . . .' or 'I am certain . . .' or 'some people are fairly sure . . .'. They are also used as a result of what is now a dying convention that a writer should not use the first person singular often, if at all. There is no doubt that many examples can be found in this book of phrases such as 'there is no doubt that . . .' when I really mean 'I am sure that . . .' (and, by implication, 'every other reasonable person would be sure too').

No statements, then, about events in the past can be described as necessarily true and if they are described as certainly true the certainty seems, on analysis, to be most accurately described as subjective. What about events in the future?

Suppose that a man has in front of him a bag containing ten white marbles. If he puts his hand in and takes one out is it not necessarily true that it will be white? Is it not completely objectively certain?

In a sense this is so, but it should be noticed that this necessity or objective certainty is hypothetical. In real life some other event might intervene to prevent the marble that was drawn out from being white; there might be a special preparation at the bottom of the bag that turned white marbles blue; they might be struck by lightning and all turned black. We can only say that *if* none of these things happen then it will be white; and we can say that it follows *necessarily* that it must be white. But this necessity is obviously the direct result of the conditions with which we have surrounded the hypothetical experiment and has therefore been put there by us in exactly the same way as the necessity with which it follows that if A = B and B = C, then A = C.

In an actual experiment a man may express himself as completely certain that the marble taken out will be white, but this is not the same thing as to say that it is objectively certain in the sense that it follows necessarily.

It happens very often for example that the majority of a conjuror's audience may feel complete certainty that a given card is the Queen of Diamonds but they find they are wrong. And it is a fact of experience that people differ widely as to the strength of evidence that is required before they will express themselves as quite certain about an event, past, present or future. Some people are naturally sceptical and cautious and never express themselves as certain about anything, while others are prepared to be convinced on the slenderest of evidence and flit wildly about from certainty to certainty however often they may be proved wrong.

It will be an aid to clear thought about this matter if we remember that the adjective 'certain' describes a state of mind· When we use phrases such as 'It is certain that . . .' we shall find on investigation and analysis that we are either describing the state of mind of one or of many people, a widely held conviction perhaps, or describing something which is necessarily true. In the latter case the necessity can only be there because we put it there.

What we described earlier as 'objective certainty' therefore is seen to be a myth arising from the way in which language is used: there is logical necessity and there is, perhaps widely held, subjective certainty. But there is nothing else.

PROBABILITY

We have talked about degrees of conviction or degrees of subjective certainty. We all know what it is to feel certain, fairly certain, doubtful, very doubtful and so on. In expressing such feelings we very often use the word 'probable,' ('I think it is probable that . . .'), but it is interesting that whereas the adjective 'certain' is applied, perhaps mainly, to a state of mind, the adjective 'probable' is applied only to something outside ourselves: '*it* is probable . . .'.

We will now consider in more detail the ways in which the word 'probable' and its derivatives are used.

Suppose that a bag contains two marbles, one white and one black, and that they are both of exactly the same size, weight and texture. If a man puts his hand into the bag and takes one out he would be said to be as likely to take out a white one as a black one, or it would be said that the chances of its being white or black are equal. Another way of expressing the same idea is to say that the *probability* of the one that is taken being black is 1/2; there are two equally likely events and taking the black marble is one of them. Suppose now that there are nine white marbles and one black one in the bag. If a man draws out one there is again no reason why any one should be taken rather than any other; there are now ten equally likely events and taking the black marble is one of them. The probability of the one that is taken being black is now said to be 1/10, and similarly the probability of its being white is 9/10. It might also be said that the chances against its being black are 9 to 1.

It is possible, of course, that if the marble is put back and the experiment is repeated several times the black marble may be drawn on the first two or three occasions consecutively in spite of the 'probability' of drawing black being 1/10. There would be a tendency then to suppose that the chances against it happening again would be greater than 9 to 1. After all, it might be argued, this improbable event has happened twice or thrice consecutively, surely it can't happen again! In fact of course the probability of drawing the black one next time is exactly the same as it was on each of the previous occasions namely 1/10: the situation is as it was, there are ten equally likely events and drawing the black marble is one of them. The probability is the same because that is the definition of probability, but of course an individual's subjective expectations about it may be very different.

The alternative to supposing that if the black marble is drawn the first three times the probability of its being drawn next time must be less than 1/10 would be to wonder whether it might be greater than 1/10. Perhaps there is after all some factor in the situation which makes it more likely that the black marble should be drawn than any of the white; perhaps the ten events are not equally likely.

'EQUALLY LIKELY'

Clearly the time has come to consider in more detail exactly what is meant by 'equally likely'. As indicated above we make the estimate that events are equally likely if we can see no reason why any one should happen rather than any other. How would we try to verify whether our estimate is correct, and what sort of test could determine whether it is correct or not?

In the example of the marbles, above, the test would be quite easy to make. We should simply set someone down to repeating the experiment a large number of times. If after 1,000 repetitions the black marble had been drawn only 50 times or more than 200 times, it would be sensible to search for reasons why it was less likely or more likely that the black marble should be taken. But if the black marble had been drawn approximately 100 times (say between 90 and 110) we should feel justified in saying that the events were equally likely and in thinking that, if we increased the number of experiments, the number of times the black marble was taken would tend to become more and more nearly equal to 1/10 of the total.

In fact the events which lend themselves to this sort of experiment are rare and usually artificial—that is they do not to any great extent happen naturally in life but have to be specially devised to illustrate what is meant by 'equally likely' or 'having a probability of 1 in 10'. In addition to marbles in bags, the tossing of coins, hands at bridge and games of chance in general provide examples where the claim that events are equally likely may be verified.

Usually when we use the phrase 'equally likely' ('It is equally likely to be wet or fine tomorrow') we apply it to the sort of event which it would be quite impossible to arrange to have repeated a large number of times and if pressed we would admit that it can only mean a subjective estimate which we make, and this estimate may or may not be founded on good evidence.

The remark about tomorrow's weather, for example, may be based on the fact that the last twenty days have contained an equal number of wet and fine days, or it may be based on the view of a meteorological expert that it is an even chance whether the depression now centred over Iceland will come our way or not.

An intricate mathematical theory of probability has been built on the assumption of equally likely events and this theory has very considerable uses. But it is important to see that what is meant by saying that A and B are equally likely to happen is either one of two things: (i) it is a claim that if the situation is repeated a large number of times, should this be possible, A will happen approximately as often as B, or (ii) the speaker is saying that he can see no reason why the one should happen rather than the other. This may be because there is very little evidence in the matter or it may be that he can see many reasons why A should happen and many reasons why B should happen but his judgement is that these reasons balance.

Useful as the Mathematical Theory of Probability undoubtedly is, it is sometimes misused and misinterpreted. It is a common error, for example, to suppose that the mathematical odds against a variety of happenings, especially unusual ones, which are not based on equally likely events, are theoretically calculable.

Suppose for example that Smith goes up to London once a year and that on two consecutive annual visits he meets by chance his old friend John Jones at Hyde Park Corner. Assuming that there is no obvious reason for this—e.g. that they were both on their way to meet their mutual friend Robinson for lunch—it would be natural for Smith to regard this as an extraordinary coincidence and to wonder perhaps what were the mathematical odds against its happening.

This would be a foolish thing to wonder, for it is not the sort of thing to which precise mathematical odds could possibly be applied. One might argue that the number of people Smith will meet (i.e. who will be close enough to be recognized) in a visit to London is, say, 5,000 and that the population of Greater London is, say, 10 million. And therefore the probability of Smith meeting any one of them, John Jones, is 5,000/10,000,000. But why Greater London? What connection is there between the number of people who live in Tooting and the likelihood of Smith meeting John Jones at Hyde Park Corner? And this fraction assumes that Smith is equally likely to meet any of the 10 million inhabitants of Greater London. How can he possibly be said to be likely to meet at Hyde Park Corner old Mrs. Green who hasn't stirred from her bed-sitting-room at Wandsworth for ten years?

Perhaps, then, instead of taking all the inhabitants of London we ought to consider only those who passed Hyde Park Corner that day. This must be a definite number, if we define 'passing Hyde Park Corner' precisely: it would be difficult to discover but we could make an estimate. But how can we say that Bill Sykes who passed Hyde Park Corner at 8.30 a.m. was 'as likely' to meet Smith as John Jones who did in fact meet him there at 12 noon?

I

Once we examine it we see that the mathematical theory of probability which is founded basically on 'equally likely' events cannot be applied.

Smith could make the experiment of going to London every day for ten years to see how often, if ever, he did 'by chance' meet John Jones at Hyde Park Corner. But though this would certainly be theoretically the most satisfactory way of producing a figure of mathematical odds, once he started to do that he would almost inevitably make estimates of the likelihood of Jones being there at certain times on certain days and those estimates could hardly fail to affect his actions.

All that one can do in a case of this kind and in the vast majority of cases where we want to know how likely it is that certain things will happen, is to make a subjective estimate. We may express the strength of this estimate by using phrases such as 'very likely', 'probably', 'unlikely' . . . or we may put it in mathematical terms by saying that we estimate the chances to be 5 to 2 on or 3 to 1 against. It may be argued that to express the strength of a subjective conviction mathematically seems to imply a precision which cannot possibly really be there. Some people would be prepared to demonstrate the genuineness of the numerical estimate which they attach to the strength of their conviction by expressing a willingness to make a bet about it. If I say 'I bet you 5 to 1 in shillings that it won't rain today' I give an indication of the strength of my conviction by saying that I am prepared to pay you 5s. if I am wrong provided that you will pay me 1s. if I am right. I estimate that the chances are 5 to 1 on. And if further pressed about what I *mean* by saying that the chances are 5 to 1, I can either simply express the same idea in slightly different words by saying that I think it is 5 times as likely not to rain as to rain, or I can say that I *mean* that my conviction about the future is such that I am prepared to bet 5 to 1 in shillings.

Clearly in an estimate of this sort one is not likely to make very subtle mathematical distinctions. It is improbable that I will go out, have another look at the weather, and then come back and announce that on reflection I now make it 16 to 3. I am much more likely to make big changes, to see a cloud on the horizon and come back and withdraw the bet, or to say that the chances are now even, or to bet that it is now going to rain.

Different people are likely to make different estimates of the same situation. Where I am prepared to bet 5 to 1 against it raining, my friend may only offer 3 to 1. This may be partly because of different states of knowledge; I listened to the weather forecast last night and he didn't, or he has seen a small cloud which I missed—in other words the evidence before us is different. Or it may be due to different interpretations which we put on the same evidence, and this may be because of a difference in experience; he has worked perhaps in a meteorological office, whereas I have no specialized skill. And the difference is also likely to be due to the fact that some people are more optimistic than others, and some people when it comes to the actual making of a bet are very much more cautious than others.

Many people would feel not only that to make a bet is morally wrong, but also that, because of this, there is something slightly sinful in expressing the strength of their conviction in betting terms. The alternative to doing so is to use necessarily vaguer adjectives, but on the other hand it may be objected that by expressing them numerically one appears to claim for the strength of one's convictions a mathematical precision to which they can hardly be entitled.

The process is a similar one in many ways to any process of evaluation. When a schoolmaster gives 7 out of 10 marks to one essay and 3 out of 10 to another he would find it hard to defend the apparent mathematical precision of the estimate he is making.

Few people would claim on reflection that the strength of our estimates can be measured with much precision, but a more accurate way of putting it would be to say that there is nothing there which is capable of precise measurement. For we must not fall into the error of supposing that the precise mathematical strength of our estimates is merely something which is concealed from us, and if only we could devise more effective and accurate methods of probing the mystery we should be able to reach a more accurate solution. The truth is that an accurate solution does not exist; our subjective estimates are necessarily vague and are not the sort of things which are capable of being expressed in precise mathematical form.

'PROBABLE' IN VARIOUS CONTEXTS

We have seen that once we accept the assumption of equally likely events a precise definition may be given of the way in which the word 'probability' is used by the Mathematicians. We have seen also that the precision which is sometimes attached to subjective estimates is only apparent.

We shall consider now contexts in which we use the words 'probable', 'probably', and we shall investigate the extent to which the probability is based on the precise mathematical theory and the extent to which it is merely a statement of a subjective estimate.

Consider, for example, the following:

(i) Jones was probably late for breakfast this morning.
(ii) He's probably on his way here at this moment.
(iii) The sun will probably shine on Harlech this afternoon
(iv) My car will probably fail to climb this hill.

It will be noticed that (i) is about the past, (ii) about the present and (iii) and (iv) are about the future.

Past events have definitely happened. Either Jones was late for breakfast this morning or he wasn't (assuming that there is a certain definite time after which Jones's arrival at the breakfast table will be described as 'late'). What do we mean by saying that he was *probably* late?

Anyone who made a remark like this would be likely to admit under cross-examination that what he really means is something like 'I should guess that Jones was late for breakfast', 'From the information at my disposal I have reason to suppose that. . . .' In other words the uncertainty expressed by 'probably' is in his mind and not in the events; there is no 'probably' about that, one way or the other it is certain.

Exactly similar arguments can obviously be applied to (ii) which is about the present: either 'He' is or is not on his way here at this moment. There can be no uncertainty in the event but only in the speaker's mind, in the state of his knowledge about it.

In both these cases although the statement is made in a form which makes the probability appear objective, it seems on examination to be really subjective.

But what about (iii) 'The sun will probably shine on Harlech this afternoon'? Is the probability or uncertainty here in the speaker's mind or, in some sense, 'in the events' and, if the latter, what do we mean by that?

Opinions might differ as to whether it is now decided whether the sun will shine on Harlech this afternoon. But most people would probably agree that with the advance of science and the increasing skill and experience of meteorologists it will be possible to forecast the future behaviour of the weather with increasing certainty and that whether the sun will shine over Harlech is a thing that is theoretically discoverable. Either it will or it won't, it may be argued. What do we mean by saying that it *probably* will?

Let us consider again what we mean when we make a more precise statement about probability, for example when we say that the probability that a certain event will happen (e.g., that a penny when tossed will land with the head uppermost) is 1/2.

We mean that if the situation (the tossing of the penny) is repeated a large number of times it will turn up 'heads' approximately 1/2 of those times. In saying that, we are not making a statement about our state of mind, the strength of our opinion as to whether it will turn up heads; we are making a statement about events, a firm clear-cut forecast of what is going to happen.

Similarly if the statement that the sun will probably shine over Harlech this afternoon is to be interpreted as a statement entirely about the events it can only mean that if a weather situation precisely similar to the present one is repeated a large number of times on future mornings the sun will shine in the afternoons more often than not. This is clearly one of those sets of experiments that can never be made thoroughly and therefore the statement can never be properly verified. (The statement would almost certainly have been based on the observation of past weather situations which were similar to varying degrees of closeness to the present one.)

But again, anyone who made this statement would be likely to admit that he is saying something about his state of mind. . . . 'I hold strongly the opinion that it will rain in Harlech this afternoon.' . . . This opinion of course would almost certainly have been based on the observation of past weather situations which were similar to varying degrees of closeness to the present one. This was the *evidence* which determined the strength of the opinion.

Statement (iv) 'My car will probably fail to climb this hill' is also about the future but it differs from (iii) in that whether the car fails or not depends not only on physical, material events—the movements of clouds, depressions, etc., but also on the human element—the skill of the driver. It would again be a matter of opinion whether it is now decided if it will fail, whether it is theoretically discoverable; but most people are probably not determinists and would therefore hold the view that it is not even theoretically now decided whether the car will fail or not.

Again, if the statement is to be interpreted as entirely about the events and not about the state of mind of the speaker, it can only mean that if the situation is repeated a large number of times the car will fail more often than not.

The experiment here would not be hard to repeat with the conditions very nearly the same at each repetition, and therefore one would have a better chance than in the preceding example of verifying the statement.

The speaker here would, if pressed, probably readily admit that he is merely expressing an opinion about what is going to happen based on past evidence ('the car failed yesterday on a hill which didn't look as steep as this').

It seems, then, that a great many of the statements we make which appear to ascribe probability to external events, which assume in other words that probability is objective, are really descriptions of our states of mind, the strength of our opinions or convictions. We all know by the most direct form of experience possible what it is to hold an opinion strongly or weakly and there is no mystery about it. It is curious that the forms of words which assume the existence of an objective probability are used much more frequently than those which explicitly describe a state of opinion. The reader will find for example in this book many more phrases like 'it is doubtful whether . . .', 'it is probably the case that . . .', than like 'I am strongly of the opinion that . . .', 'most people doubt whether . . .'. This is an example of our thinking being determined to some extent by the forms of words which we have inherited. As long as we are aware of this and are prepared by careful analysis to discover what we really mean, it may not greatly matter. But if we fail to do these things there is a danger that our thoughts may become the slaves of our words instead of the masters of them.

Whether we say that an event is certain or probable, the strength of our conviction or opinion, is determined obviously by a consideration of the evidence.

We all know in a general way what we mean by evidence and how we consider it but it is important to give this matter rather closer attention. We will do so in the next chapter.

Examples on Chapter 7

1. Comment on the uses of the words italicized in the following passages:

(i) The Throgmorton Thursday football team is *certain* to win the cup.

(ii) It is *certain* that if you move your king there, Robinson will be able to mate you in two moves.

(iii) Since you only hold one Premium Bond the *probability* is that you won't get any prize for the next five years.

(iv) The Conservatives will *probably* win the next Election.

(v) 'Although some government spokesmen affect to think otherwise, *there is not a shadow of a doubt* that the Jordan Government has the support of only a fraction of the population.'

(*Spectator*, 1 August, 1958)

(vi) 'The initiative of some banks in offering loans for domestic expenditures more readily is intended among other things to attract new customers from groups who hitherto have not had bank accounts. *It is certain* to impinge on normal hire purchase business, because hire purchase facilities are widely used by people who already have bank accounts.'

(*The Times*, 28 August, 1958)

(vii) 'It is, for example, *almost certain* that we cannot get our troops out of Jordan without U.N. help.'

(*Spectator*, 25 July, 1958)

(viii) 'There is *probably* not much to choose between the two answers in cost when the implications are fully analysed. . . .

'To fly a vehicle direct from England is *probably not* more expensive than to store and maintain two or three of its kind overseas for a period of years. . . .

'As the number of freighter aircraft Britain would require would be small, it would *probably* be more economical, and *certainly* quicker, to buy them from America than to build them here. . . .

'But it is *probably* too late now to unscramble the organization.'

(*The Times*, 27 August, 1958)

2. In a country there are 5 million different car numbers: these numbers are all put in a large container and 100 of them are drawn out. What can you say about the chances of any given number being amongst these 100?

If you go for a drive in this country and meet 100 different cars what can you say about the chances of any given number being amongst these 100?

3. Consider the following arguments:

(i) If a penny is tossed it will either come down heads or tails: the probability of its coming down heads is therefore 1/2.

(ii) If two pennies are tossed they will either both come down heads or they won't: the probability of their both coming down heads is therefore 1/2.

(iii) If three pennies are tossed the result will be either three heads, two heads and a tail, two tails and a head, or three tails: the probability of three heads is therefore 1/4.

(iv) If you go for a walk this afternoon either you will meet Bill Bloggs or you won't: the probability of your meeting him is therefore 1/2.

(v) In a Telephone Directory there are 40,000 different entries and 15,000 different names. If an entry is taken at random, therefore, the probability of his having a given name is 1/15,000.

(vi) There are 10 different Doctors in this town. If you get run over by a bus, therefore, the probability of your being treated by any one of them is 1/10.

8

Induction

In this chapter we shall be exclusively concerned with what we have called 'open' systems of thinking, that is to say with thoughts and statements and processes of reasoning which are concerned with the world around us, the world of experience. We shall consider how we arrive at such statements and conclusions, the sort of questions that might be asked about them and how they would be answered, and the sort of support in the shape of evidence or argument that might be produced for them. To do all this is to investigate the processes of Induction and the nature of cause and effect, considerably more thoroughly than we did in an earlier chapter.

If we were to regard the events that happen to us and around us as isolated and disconnected we should look at the world as a chaotic and senseless muddle. It is the desire to produce order out of chaos that impels us to search for regularities and connections, to docket things and label them. We are going to investigate now some of the ways in which our minds handle the material that our senses lay before us, for it is obvious that all our knowledge of the external world comes to us through sense experience. The reader is in one sense already familiar with such processes; he is inevitably for a large part of his waking life sifting and collating the evidence provided by his senses, although he may usually be doing it unreflectively. We are all of us also inevitably hearing and reading about the results of such processes performed by other people.

We will now consider some specific statements of regularities.

(1) 'Most negroes have curly hair.'

The general reaction to this statement would probably be one of agreement. Most of us have seen enough negroes in real life or in photographs or pictures to be able to form an opinion that it is true. And this is clearly the sort of simple evidence that is required—the examination of a large number of particular cases and the discovery that in a majority of them the statement is true. We may thus come to the conclusion, based on a study of the evidence, that these two characteristics—of being a negro and of having curly hair—are often found together (we must not say *usually* for though we may be agreed that most negroes have curly hair there may not be evidence to show that most people with curly hair are negroes). Such characteristics may therefore be called Concomitant.

Someone who was coming across this bit of information for the first time, however, would be very likely to ask *Why*. 'I don't see', he might say, 'why negroes should have curly hair. What's it due to?'

What sort of answer would he expect to this question? Would it satisfy him if we say 'Well, you see, they are concomitant characteristics'? It would not be very sensible of him to be so easily satisfied, and the fact that he has asked the questions makes it likely that what he is searching for is some causal connection between these two characteristics. The sort of explanation that would satisfy him might be something on these lines: 'The black skin of a negro is due to a pigmentation-formation of the skin tissue which is Nature's way of protecting the skin from the extreme heat of the sun. This same pigmentation forms a hard layer on the scalp and the hairs of the young negro can only force themselves through it by adopting a corkscrew motion, and they retain this shape in after life even though the purpose for which it was adopted has been achieved.'

Or perhaps he might be satisfied by an explanation of this

type: 'It is when it is in a curly formation that hair provides the maximum protection for a given quantity against the rays of the sun. And just as Nature provides the negro with a dark skin to protect him from the sun so also she provides him with curly hair for the same purpose.'

Notice an important difference between these two 'explanations'. In the first, one of the characteristics (having a black skin) is shown to be the cause of the other; the black skin comes first and produces, is responsible for, the curly hair. In the second explanation both the characteristics are said to be due to the same cause, but that cause is of a different kind; the black skin and the curly hair are both there for a purpose, the same purpose, in order that there shall be protection from the sun. Other people who held different views about the nature of evolution might want to say that the two characteristics are both caused by the climate in the other sense of *cause*, and that the idea of purpose does not enter into it.

We have given these explanations as types to illustrate a point; whether they are true or not does not for the moment matter. But for these particular concomitant characteristics it may well be that for most people no further explanation would be necessary. Unless they are unusually inquisitive or happen to be investigating racial characteristics most people would accept the fact as given, from observation or from hearsay, and would be content to think—if they think about it at all—that these characteristics just are found together. It may not be possible to give a reason either because none exists or because our knowledge of the matter is not yet sufficiently advanced.

Let us consider now another statement:

(2) 'Most knock-kneed people have blue eyes.'

Our first reaction to this statement is likely to be one of disbelief. We should certainly want to be shown evidence that this was true in a large number of particular cases, but even if this were done we should still be likely to feel uncertain. Perhaps the cases have been specially selected, perhaps it has been a series of extraordinary coincidences. There would still be the feeling that if we go and select a random knock-kneed person he is no more likely than anybody else to have blue eyes. We should be likely to ask for supporting reasons, to demand *why* this should be so. The answer that it just is, that being knock-kneed and having blue eyes are concomitant characteristics would be less likely to satisfy us than it would in the case of the negroes and the curly hair. We are less ready to be convinced by the enumeration of particular cases, we want other kinds of evidence because, perhaps, the proposition strikes us to start with as being so improbable. Why is this so?

One answer is because in the first case of concomitant characteristics most of us are familiar with at least one instance and we are less likely to search for reasons for events, or for connections and conjunctions of characteristics with which we have personal acquaintance.

A second answer is because the characteristics mentioned are the kind of physical characteristic which we recognize to be quite often found in association.

Whether or no we have direct experience of negroes having curly hair, we have probably associated Italians with dark hair and eyes, yellow-skinned people with smallness of stature, Scandinavians with fair hair and blue eyes. We recognize that there are certain physical characteristics like colour of skin, hair, eyes, which are commonly found together and the declaration of another association of this kind is not likely to appear particularly surprising.

But to be knock-kneed and to have blue eyes are hardly both to be thought of as racial characteristics, we have certainly never noticed them as being concomitant and if we were partially convinced of the truth of the statement by the enumeration of many cases we should certainly be likely to want to find a reason. To say 'They just are' would be for most of us a highly unsatisfactory conclusion of the matter.

The sort of answer that might satisfy us would be one that associated having knock-knees with the Scandinavian races because, say, of certain athletic pursuits or exercises which were popular with young people there, and as the association of blue eyes with the Scandinavian races is a well-known one a *reason* for the statement would thus be provided.

A more convincing example of the same kind of reason is provided by the statement:

(3) 'Most bull-fighters are dark-eyed.'

Even though one has never in fact met a bull-fighter one would have no difficulty in seeing a reason why this is probably true. It is unlikely that being a bull-fighter makes a man's eyes go dark or that having dark eyes makes one especially disposed to fight bulls. It is unlikely, in other words, that either characteristic is the cause of the other. It is well known however that most bull-fighters are Spaniards and that most Spaniards have dark eyes: both characteristics therefore can be attributed to the same cause, namely being a Spaniard.

(It is hoped that the alert reader will have noticed that the syllogism:

'Most Spaniards are dark-eyed;

Most bull-fighters are Spaniards;

∴ most bull-fighters are dark-eyed,'

is not in fact a valid one as the middle term is undistributed in both premisses. Whether the conclusion follows depends of course on the strength of the 'most's, on just how large a proportion they cover. The present writer's, admittedly secondhand, information on the subject leads him to believe that the proportions are large enough to justify the conclusion.)

(4) 'Tall people can see more easily in crowds.'

For this statement no evidence, reason or support would be needed for most people. Once it is known what it is to be tall and once one has had experience of seeing or trying to see in crowds it is quite clear that the first characteristic is the *cause* of the second. No enumeration of a large number of cases would be necessary, and it is only a very obstinate or stupid person who would persist in asking *Why*. Although the two characteristics—of being tall and of being able to see more easily in crowds—are found together and are therefore strictly speaking *concomitant* it is not of this kind of example that the phrase is normally used.

(5) 'Left-handed people are better at Chinese.'

This statement is like the second one in that it might at first sight appear rather improbable. If we were told that most Chinese were left-handed we should not find that particularly surprising. Without knowing whether it is true or what reasons there might be for it, there would be no great difficulty in thinking of possible reasons—for example that as a matter of religion or custom the young in China are trained to use their left hands almost exclusively in their early days. But to state that what most people would regard as the accident of being left-handed is always associated with a particular mental skill—and one which not many people have the opportunity of testing—is at least surprising. As with the example of the knock-kneed we should want the enumeration of a very large number of cases to convince us, and even then we should quite likely not be entirely satisfied and might search still for a reason why.

The sort of reason that might prove satisfying is that as the Chinese write from right to left a left-handed person writing Chinese is in a similar situation to a right-handed person writing English, and since he finds it easier to write (as the back-handed motion is intrinsically easier than the fore-handed), he will find it easier to learn and will therefore, other things being equal, be better at it.

There are, then, different kinds of support which might be produced for these statements. There is first of all the *evidence* that the statement is true in each case, the sort of evidence that is provided by producing or quoting a large number of particular instances which exemplify the statement. And there is secondly the support provided by *reasons* why the statement should be true. These reasons may take the form of showing that one characteristic causes the other, or that both characteristics are due to some common cause. There is a tendency sometimes to forget this latter possibility. When cancer of the lung is found to occur more often among smokers than among non-smokers the most obvious interpretation is that smoking is at least a contributory cause of the disease. It has, however, been suggested as an alternative explanation that the kind of person who has an urge to smoke in order to soothe his nerves is likely to be predisposed to cancer of the lung, that the two characteristics in other words may both be due to a common cause.

The more obvious and convincing is the support provided by the reasons why the characteristics should appear together, the less necessary it is likely to be to produce evidence by simple enumeration. And it is also often true that the more common are the instances of the association, the more familiar in other words the individual is with the concomitance in question, the less likely he is to want to know *why* the characteristics should be found together.

WHY

One important point that has emerged from the above examples is that answers to 'Why' questions may be of more than one kind. If I am asked why I went to Hereford yesterday my answer might be that it was because my Uncle James took me there or it might be that it was because I wanted to see the Cathedral. These are both reasons and perfectly good ones but they are not reasons of the same sort. The first reason is of the kind that one most often associates with cause and effect. I went because I was taken, in the same way that a cricket ball goes to the boundary because a batsman struck it with his bat. This kind of cause is sometimes called an *efficient* cause. It might also be called a *mechanical* cause. It is when something happens as a result of a preceding event and it is of a kind that we see operating daily when we press buttons, pull levers, hit golf-balls, wash our hands, brush our hair or watch a wave sweep a piece of wood on to the rocks.

The second reason is in terms of purpose; I went to Hereford for the purpose of seeing, in order to see, the Cathedral. This kind of cause is called a *final* cause. It is only people and not machines that can have purposes so that when I ask why my car won't go I am likely to be in search of an efficient rather than a final cause. (Unless I take the view that it does it to annoy me.) But when one asks someone 'Why did you do that?' one is more likely to be asking him for what purpose he did it. The kind of answer that the enquirer is expecting will usually be clear from the context.

In the example about my going to Hereford both the suggested reasons may in a sense be true. But if I had the overriding purpose to see the Cathedral and I bent my Uncle James to my will and compelled him to drive me there, it would be proper to describe him taking me there as *how* I went to Hereford rather than *why*. If, however, I have always wanted to see the Cathedral and I knew that my Uncle was going there that afternoon, then both reasons would be likely to appear relevant to my questioner.

It should be noticed that all answers to '*Why?*' questions that are asked about the world of experience must, if they are to be satisfactory, be of one of these two types or possibly a mixture of the two: they must either give a cause or causes which pro-

K

duced the occurrence or a purpose or purposes for which it was done or possibly both. But no other satisfactory sort of answer is possible. A kind of answer which is sometimes given and which may appear different is the statement of a general rule. Thus if I ask 'Why does this fall to the ground when I let go of it?' I might be told that all bodies do if there is nothing to stop them, but this would hardly count as a satisfactory explanation. But if I ask why the shops are shut this afternoon and am told that they always are on Wednesdays because that is early closing day, I would feel that the matter has been satisfactorily explained. I have been told the general rule into which the object of my enquiry fits, but that rule is not simply a generalization derived from observing the facts, it is a regulation or agreement which may justly be said to be the *cause* of the shops being shut this afternoon in a way in which the answer that they always do can hardly be said to be the cause of bodies falling to the ground.

The idea that some explanation of events may be possible other than an efficient or a final cause is often responsible for much muddle-headed and necessarily fruitless enquiry.

The answers to 'Why' questions in closed systems of thinking will of course take the form of logical reasons. The answer to the question: 'Why is the square on the hypotenuse of a right-angled triangle equal to the sum of the squares on the other two sides?' is the proof of the theorem of Pythagoras. If the questioner does not find this answer satisfactory but persists in asking Why, it would be necessary to explain the proofs of all the theorems which precede Pythagoras.

CAUSE AND EFFECT

The idea of cause and effect has hitherto been taken for granted as most people do in their ordinary daily lives. Most of us probably think that we know in a general way what we mean by it, but would not find easy the task of explaining it clearly in detail.

We are now going to examine and analyse the idea more closely. Throughout this section the causes we shall be considering, unless we specifically state otherwise, will be those we have called *efficient* causes.

Let us take an example.

I get into my car and pull the self-starter: the engine leaps into life.

Why?

If I had to explain this to someone who doubted that they were connected and wanted to know more about the nature of the connection, if any; what sort of answer would I give? Would I produce evidence by simple enumeration? This, I'm afraid, would not be very convincing for in fact if I come to examine the precise statistics of it I find that my pulling the self-starter is more often followed by curious noises and the engine not leaping into life. But yet I am quite convinced, and so are you who read this, that when the car does start after I have pulled the starter the one event was caused by the other. And in any case even if it happened every time, thus making the simple enumeration method more convincing, that would merely be to produce evidence for the fact that *A* is always followed by *B*, not to give a reason *why* that should be so or to explain what it is to 'cause'.

In order to explain why the one event is followed by the other I would have to know something about the Internal Combustion Engine and my explanation would be much easier and clearer if I were allowed to point and show as well as to talk.

It might start something like this:

'You see that there is a wire attached to this knob, and the other end of the wire is fastened to a lever which therefore moves in this direction when the knob is pulled . . . , etc.'

What has to be done clearly is to examine the chain of events, of causes and effects, as it were through a microscope, to describe all the intermediate happenings, the *immediate* effect of pulling the knob and then the immediate effect of that effect and so on. The chain is taken to pieces, analysed and examined, and for most people, for most purposes, that would be enough. I would be said to have 'explained' why pulling that knob starts the engine if I have described in detail the events which occur between the one happening and the other. It might also be said that I have described *how* the car starts and this illustrates the point that to answer a *how* and a *why* question may sometimes be very nearly the same thing.

But suppose someone is not satisfied. Suppose he says: '*Why?* I don't see why just because you pull this wire and it's fastened to something at the other end, the thing at the other end should move too.'

What answer can we make to him? Can we say that it follows *necessarily* as with cases of deductive argument? Can we say that it is inconceivable that it shouldn't be so?

Clearly not the latter for the wire might break, or it might stretch in such a way that the other end did not move.

But can we not say that *if* the wire doesn't break, and *if* it's inelastic then it is inconceivable that the other end should not move, that it follows necessarily that it must, and if our friend is unable to see that he must be very stupid or very obstinate or perhaps, as in a deductive example earlier, he is insufficiently acquainted with the terms involved? We had better introduce him to a few more wires.

When we make the statement hedged about with so many qualifications it might be argued that we are making it a necessary statement by putting the necessity in; that we are saying in effect that if the wire is of such a kind that the other end will move when I pull this end, then if nothing happens to prevent it doing so the other end *will* move when I pull this. We can couch the statement in such a form that it carries with it necessity or theoretical certainty, but the events which are being described are the events of experience. The fact that, usually, if we pull one end of a wire the other end moves is derived from experience and it is a fact which we come to see and absorb very early in life. As soon as we start touching or seeing material objects we experience events similar to this. And to the question *Why* it should happen no answer seems possible except that it just does. It is to events of this kind, the simplest sort of link in the chain of cause and effect, that all chains can be reduced and in terms of which they can all be explained. When we are investigating or analysing we want to postpone for as long as possible the answer 'It just does—it's a fact of experience—look around you and see'. And indeed one of the main points of an investigation, of asking a 'why' or a 'how' question, is to discover more intermediate links. But the answer 'It just does' is bound to come eventually.

A search for the ultimate nature of the causal link is bound to be puzzling. But there is no doubt that we derive the idea of causation from experience, from observing a large number of instances in which *A* is followed by *B*. To attempt to discover more about the nature of the connection in general, if indeed there is more to be discovered, is a matter for the student of Philosophy and would be out of place here.

THE SEARCH FOR CAUSAL CONNECTIONS

Our search for causal connections is not likely to be at all impeded by our failure to understand the precise philosophical nature of the causal link. This search for regularities and for causes and effects is taking place the whole time as we have pointed out earlier. One object of the search is to enable us to arrange our knowledge tidily, to produce the order of explanation out of the chaos of unrelated events. But an even more important result is that we are enabled to *predict*, to foretell what is going to happen next time—what will be the result of heating that liquid, what time the moon will rise, how heavy a load that steel bar will carry. And if we are able to predict we are thereby enabled also to plan ahead, to control our environment, to assert a mastery over Nature. *Prediction* and *Planning* are the main objects of Science and the Scientific Method.

In the example which we recently considered of the motor car being started, there was no difficulty for someone who had learnt about it in discovering what were the causes of certain effects. Unless it had been known how events of the type which occurred between the pulling of the self-starter and the starting of the car were causally connected, the car could never have been designed and built.

Let us consider now—and this is a very important part of our thinking about the world around us—the discovery of causes and effects rather than the description of them.

In an elementary way this sort of discovery is simply organized common sense. If I find that whenever A happens it is always accompanied by or followed by B and that B never occurs without A then we are justified in saying that A and B are causally connected. If I find that my going upstairs is accompanied by a distinctive squeaking noise I might make further experiments to discover what causes it. I might find that the squeak is absent if I miss out the third stair from the top and further investigation might show that it is absent unless there is pressure on a certain part of this stair. Trial and error show that pressure here is always accompanied by the squeak and that the squeak never occurs unless there is pressure here (or we might say that the pressure is a sufficient and necessary condition for the squeak). And therefore we say that the pressure causes the squeak.

This kind of common-sense procedure for the discovery of causes is familiar to all of us. It has been expressed more formally and in more detail by J. S. Mill and other logicians but it must in effect be reducible to a method of this kind.

If we want to know what causes a squeak we examine various

examples of its occurrence and the accompanying circumstances. Those circumstances which always accompany the squeak are likely to contain its cause, and as we narrow down the search for a cause and suspect that it may lie in a certain particular item 'p' we make two experiments in which the accompanying circumstances are exactly the same except for the presence or absence of 'p' (in this case stepping on the third stair from the top). If in one experiment the squeak occurs and in the other it does not then we regard it as highly probable that the squeak was caused by 'p'. Theoretically we could regard it as certain but in practice it would be difficult to ensure that the experiments were *exactly* the same except for 'p', and we should be sensible to make further tests by concentrating our attention and our pressure on the third stair from the top.

This method of searching for causes is of course a commonplace of scientific enquiry, and the controlled experiment, where the conditions are repeated with just the alteration of one item which is suspected of being a significant one, is used continually wherever it is possible. It is the method by which we gradually discover the item or items which are always present when the effect does occur, and always absent when it doesn't.

We must notice, however, that although the same cause always produces the same effect—(that is based on the assumption of the uniformity of Nature, an assumption that is derived from the observation of Nature)—a given effect may in general be produced by a variety of causes. If I catch the 2.46 train from Winchester and don't get out on the way then I shall be at Waterloo at 4.15, but from the fact that I am at Waterloo at 4.15 we cannot argue with certainty that I must have caught the 2.46 from Winchester. This is an example of the fact which we have noticed earlier that from 'If p, then q' we are *not* entitled to infer 'But q, $\therefore p$'. What we can say, however, is 'If $\bar{q}$, then $\bar{p}$'. If we suspect that p is always followed by q our theory is supported but not proved by cases of q following p; it would not be disproved by q occurring not preceded by p, but it would be disproved by q not occurring after p.

Clearly on any particular occasion a given effect must have resulted from a definite cause or set of causes. But whereas on different occasions the same set of causes must produce the same effect, it is not true to say that the same effect must be produced by the same set of causes. If for example the distributor falls out of my car on Monday, Tuesday and Wednesday the car will stop on each occasion, but if my car stops on Monday, Tuesday and Wednesday the cause might be different each time.

It is possible and sometimes useful to represent the procedure of searching for causes in shorthand form.

Suppose for example that the letters $A, B, C \ldots p, q, r \ldots$, etc. stand for events or conditions and the arrow $\longrightarrow$ stands for 'is followed by'.

Suppose that the results of various experiments are represented thus:

(i) $\left.\begin{array}{c} A \\ B \\ C \\ D \\ E \end{array}\right\} \longrightarrow p, q, r, s$ (ii) $\left.\begin{array}{c} A \\ D \end{array}\right\} \longrightarrow r$

(iii) $\left.\begin{array}{c} B \\ C \\ D \end{array}\right\} \longrightarrow p, s$ (iv) $\left.\begin{array}{c} A \\ D \\ E \end{array}\right\} \longrightarrow q, r$

(v) $\left.\begin{array}{c} A \\ B \\ D \end{array}\right\} \longrightarrow r, s$

What conclusions can we come to about possible causal links?

We will suppose that we want to find possible causes for p, and in doing so we must remember that the same cause must always have the same effect, but the same effect may be due to a variety of causes. The fact that p occurs in (i) and (iii) enables us to infer merely that all the 5 events, A, B, C, D, E may be causes of p. The fact that in (iii) p occurs when A is absent does not entitle us to infer that A is not a cause of p, as can perhaps be seen more clearly by considering that the fact that my car stops when the petrol feed is not blocked does not entitle us to infer that the blocking of the petrol feed would not cause my car to stop.

It will be more helpful in the above example if we consider the situations where p does not occur in order to find the events which could not have caused it. An examination of (ii), (iv), (v) shows that none of the items A, B, D, E can by themselves be causes of p for, if they were, p would be present when they were present. We thus come to the conclusion that C is the only possible single cause.

(If the experiments are of a kind which make it possible that two or more of the events A, B, C, D, E may be the joint cause of p the situation would be rather different. Further experiments would be necessary to exhaust the possibilities.)

The reader should check for himself that similar arguments show E to be a possible cause of q, A or E of r (with A the more likely as whenever r occurs it is always preceded by A, but as E is never present when r is absent we cannot rule out the possibility that E may always be followed by r), and B or C of s with, by a similar argument, B the more likely.

It is only possible to make these controlled experiments in certain sciences or lines of enquiry. The Physicist, the Chemist, the Engineer and to some extent the Biologist can do it: they have their laboratories and over a considerable field of their enquiries it is possible for them to make a series of experiments in which the conditions are altered each time to an extent which is entirely under the control of the experimenter; the variables in the experiment are usually of a specific kind and limited in number and they can be adjusted at will.

The Economist, the Psychologist and the Social Scientist in general, however, are in a very different position. It is hard for them to make experiments, their variables are large in number and indefinite in kind and in a great number of cases it is not possible for the experimenter to control them.

They are also to a very considerable extent dealing with final causes, the purposes of human beings, as well as with efficient ones. It is obvious that these are not only harder to control but also very much more difficult to discover.

In both cases, the exact sciences and the less exact ones, it is always possible for the cause to be not a single isolated event but a combination of several events; this however is more likely to be so in the less exact sciences.

Just as there is a danger which we noted earlier of the Logician confining himself to examples of reasoning where the results are certain and the logic two-valued, Yes or No, Black or White, so there is a danger that only those fields of enquiry in which controlled experiments are possible, in which results are measurable, in which cause and effect can be clearly traced and the causes are likely to be simple rather than complex, will be thought worthy of the name of '*Science*'.

Happily both these points of view are now less widely held, for to hold them is to close the avenues of enquiry into vast realms of human experience.

EMPIRICAL GENERALIZATIONS

We have said that our search for chains of cause and effect is one of the results of our desire to produce order out of chaos, to docket and label and connect the events which we experience and to recognize and card-index the regularities which we find in the world.

The mere statement of regularities in a generalized form may simply be the statement of concomitant characteristics—e.g. all ravens are black—and such statements are empirical generalizations. Unless blackness is included in what it is to be a raven, i.e. part of the definition of a raven (in which case of course the statement would be analytic), it would be impossible to be quite certain about this generalization in its most sweeping form, but nevertheless it is one that might be made with a high degree of confidence. As we have seen, such generalizations are built up from the consideration of a large number of particular cases and they form the basis and an essential part of the method of certain kinds of scientific enquiry. Research workers in Natural History and to a considerable extent in the social sciences are collecting and building up generalizations of this kind from many separate instances. ('The eggs of cockroaches take three or four months to hatch', 'People go to pubs to have a drink', 'More men under thirty smoke cigarettes than pipes.') Their object in doing so may just be the acquisition of knowledge for curiosity's sake, it may be to enable them to predict future happenings in order to plan and control events, or it may be to advance the cause of knowledge further by constructing a basis for a Scientific Hypothesis.

SCIENTIFIC HYPOTHESES

Regularities in the world around us are observed, noted and collected. Partly by observation and common sense and partly by the more rigorous method of the controlled experiment the causal links between happenings are discovered. In a great many cases the regularities are obvious, and they are the ones which are expressed as empirical generalizations. Very often, however, in a series of events it may be clear that there is a regularity there and easy to express it in a vague form, but difficult to express it in the more precise form which will make accurate prediction possible.

It was not difficult, for example, to arrive at the generalization that most bodies fall to the ground if there is no object in the way to stop them. At one time it was thought that the answer to the question why they should do this was because they wanted to get to the centre of the earth. This was an interesting theory but not one that enlarged the scope or the accuracy of prediction beyond that provided by the original generalization.

There are various regularities of movement that can be observed when things are left to themselves—stones falling from the tops of cliffs, planets moving about in the skies—and when a hypothesis is constructed about the principles according to which they move, the Theory of Gravitation, we have discovered something about the form which the regularities take.

The usefulness of this theory and its validity depend on the extent to which it increases the scope and accuracy of our predictions. It is well known that on this account the Theory of Gravitation has been remarkably successful.

To think of, construct or invent a scientific hypothesis, then, is to describe the form of the observed regularities. The data for such hypotheses are the empirical generalizations but to form the hypothesis is to take a considerably more difficult step and a step, as it were, on a more advanced plane than that of the generalization itself.

The hypothesis may take the form of a mathematical or scientific equation connecting the variables or it may merely express a new and productive way of looking at things. Its test is that it should fit the data as far as they are known and that it should enable us to predict with increased certainty and accuracy.

A scientific hypothesis is thus seen to be not merely the culmination of a process of induction in which one is arguing from the particular to the more and more general: it is a process of another and more advanced kind.

SUMMARY

Not many of us are likely to be in a position to form scientific hypotheses but we can all endeavour to think straight about the world around us, and examine critically the conclusions about it at which other people arrive.

In this chapter we have covered a lot of ground and have inevitably dealt rather superficially with some of the fundamental questions which have been raised. It is hoped, however, that the reader will be more likely to explain things properly himself and assess correctly the worth of the explanations of others if he understands something of the nature of explanation. Similarly he is more likely to detect and to analyse chains of cause and effect if he has investigated the principles on which they are based.

The strength of the evidence for empirical statements may often be a difficult thing to assess, but we are more likely to do it successfully if we understand how generalizations are built up—by simple enumeration or on the basis of causal links—and we must be prepared always to examine and criticize the evidence, to ask Why, and to understand when it no longer makes sense to ask Why. All these things are really matters of common sense and they are also part of the scientific method, but they are regrettably not always a part of the thinking habits of the ordinary man.

Examples on Chapter 8

1. Would you expect the person who asked the following questions to be in search of an efficient or a final cause or both? Comment in each case, if you think it relevant, on the context in which they might be asked.

    (i) Why is it colder at the North Pole than at the Equator?
    (ii) Why did you miss that ball?

   (iii) Why is the grass so long here?

   (iv) Why are you late?

   (v) Why have you left the butter in the sun?

   (vi) Why is your horse lame?

  (vii) Why can't you stand up straight?

 (viii) Why is there so much suffering in the world?

   (ix) Why are ravens black?

   (x) Why is water wet?

2. The letters $A, B, C, D, E, p, q, r, x, y, z$ stand for events. The sign $\longrightarrow$ means 'are followed by'.

It is known that the events p, q, r, x, y, z have as their causes single events, not two or more events in conjunction; though it is possible for q, for example, to be caused by either A or D. What happens can be represented as follows:

(i) $\left.\begin{array}{l} A \\ B \\ C \end{array}\right\} \longrightarrow p, q$
   (ii) $\left.\begin{array}{l} B \\ D \\ E \end{array}\right\} \longrightarrow q, r$
   (iii) $\left.\begin{array}{l} B \\ C \\ D \end{array}\right\} \longrightarrow p, r$

(iv) $\left.\begin{array}{l} A \\ B \\ E \end{array}\right\} \longrightarrow q$
   (v) $\left.\begin{array}{l} p \\ q \end{array}\right\} \longrightarrow y, z$
   (v) $\left.\begin{array}{l} q \\ r \end{array}\right\} \longrightarrow x$

What can you say about the chains of cause and effect which connect the various events? Give as complete an answer as you can.

3. The letters A, B, C, D, E and $p, q, r, s, t, a, b, c, d, e$ stand for events. The sign $\longrightarrow$ means 'are followed by'.

(i) $\left.\begin{array}{l} A \\ B \\ C \\ D \\ E \end{array}\right\} \longrightarrow p, q, r, s, t$
   (ii) $\left.\begin{array}{l} A \\ B \\ E \end{array}\right\} \longrightarrow s, t$

(iii) $\left.\begin{array}{l} B \\ C \\ D \end{array}\right\} \longrightarrow r, s$
   (iv) $\left.\begin{array}{l} A \\ C \\ D \\ E \end{array}\right\} \longrightarrow p, q, s$

(v) $\left.\begin{array}{l} p \\ r \\ t \end{array}\right\} \!\!\longrightarrow\! b, c, d$ (vi) $\left.\begin{array}{l} p \\ q \\ t \end{array}\right\} \!\!\longrightarrow\! a, d, e$

(vii) $\left.\begin{array}{l} r \\ s \\ t \end{array}\right\} \!\!\longrightarrow\! a, c, e$ (viii) $\left.\begin{array}{l} p \\ q \\ r \\ s \end{array}\right\} \!\!\longrightarrow\! a, b, d$

(ix) $\left.\begin{array}{l} q \\ s \\ t \end{array}\right\} \!\!\longrightarrow\! b, d, e$

The situations are such that it is possible for single events or for two or more events in conjunction to cause subsequent events.

You are faced with a situation where the events A, B, C, D, E would normally be happening but you have it in your power to prevent any of them. How would you prevent c from happening with the minimum of interference with A, B, C, D, E? Justify your answer.

4. A certain machine is subject from time to time to three faults: the widgets wumble, the stugs stick and the sprockets fall off.
The following observations are made:

When the lid is taken off, button B is pressed and the lever marked Forward is pulled back, the engine boils and the anemometer quivers.

The pressing of button B, the removal of the safety catch and a firm tap on the plate C, marked DO NOT TOUCH, are accompanied by a quivering anemometer and the input register turning blue.

If the lid is taken off, plate C tapped and the Forward lever pulled back the engine boils, and the input register turns blue.

When the safety catch is removed, plate C tapped and the Forward lever pulled back the input register turns blue.

When the engine boils and the input register turns blue, the widgets wumble.

If the anemometer quivers and the input register turns blue the stugs stick and the sprockets fall off.

On the basis of this data what would you do or not do to cure the machine of each of its faults? Justify your answer.

5. It has been suggested that there is a connection between the

number of rabbits and the amount of ragwort. The following are extracts from an article about it in *The Times* and from correspondence which followed:

(i) 'This has been a bad season for ragwort' (i.e. there has been a lot of it). 'Some farmers think that this is because of the absence of rabbits which kept down the ragwort in its early stages of growth.'

(The Times, 26 August, 1957)

(ii) '... I have paid special attention to the problem of ragwort and cannot agree with the statements in your Farming Notes and Comments of August 26.

'Rabbits did not eat many of the young seedlings of ragwort, which abounded in the short turf which they grazed ...... the amount of ragwort has become very small, as shown by the colour photographs which I take at the same spots each August. ... Places which used to be bare chalk rubble with a mass of ragwort are now covered with grass in which grow a few stunted ragwort plants ... ... the indications are that should the rabbits return in large quantities, so also would this pernicious poisonous weed. ...'

(The Times, 30 August, 1957)

(iii) '... Since myxomatosis ragwort has become notably less prolific, and when your correspondent writes "Places which used to be bare chalk rubble with a mass of ragwort are now covered with grass ...", I think he has the explanation. ... ragwort ... its natural enemy, grass.'

(The Times, 2 September, 1957)

What do you think is the 'explanation' referred to in the last paragraph? Describe clearly the suggested causal connections between rabbits and ragwort. On the evidence supplied by these extracts which do you think is most likely?

6. The number of people convicted of smuggling goods into this country to evade paying duty is shown below.

1950–51	-	-	2,293
1952–53	-	-	1,647
1953–54	-	-	1,311
1955–56	-	-	1,123

Suggest reasons for the decrease.

9

Errors and Deceptions in Reasoning

IN our attempts to describe and explain correct methods of reasoning we have inevitably touched from time to time on methods of reasoning which are incorrect. We propose in this chapter to deal rather more systematically with the accidental mistakes and the deliberate attempts to deceive which may occur in our thinking and argument.

Every piece of reasoning that is expressed in words either written or spoken is so expressed with a definite purpose. It will be useful to consider what the possible purposes are.

They can broadly be classified under two headings:
(1) To arrive at the truth or to communicate the truth.
(2) To persuade, to score debating points, to get the better of someone in an argument.

To classify our purposes under these two main headings is not to say, of course, that they are mutually exclusive. In fact, as we shall suggest, in a very large number of cases our motives are consciously or unconsciously a mixture of the two.

If our thinking, as expressed either on paper or in discussion, is genuinely designed to help ourselves or others to arrive at the truth, then any mistakes there may be in the reasoning will certainly not be deliberate. They will arise from a genuine muddle, from stupidity, or from the fact that we have not been taught how to avoid them; they will either be mistakes in logic or they will be errors due to the fact that unconsciously we are allowing our thinking to be influenced by our emotions. This latter reason operates perhaps more often than we like to think.

L

It is not hard to think of extreme cases of the second classification where we are frankly trying to persuade or to score points. It is quite customary for people to support in a debate a motion in which they do not entirely believe. Though it would certainly not be thought legitimate in such circumstances to produce statements which are known not to be true, it would be common practice to suppress facts which do not support the case that is being argued. Most debaters also would not be too scrupulous about the validity of the reasoning they employed, and would certainly not refrain from appealing to emotions, convention, habit, prestige, self-interest, if by doing so they thought it likely that they would advance their cause. The object of the exercise is quite openly to make the best case possible for the motion for which one is speaking, and to persuade those who are listening to vote for it. The fact that obvious mistakes of reasoning, appeals to emotion or unfair argument are likely to be exposed by the opposition, or perhaps spotted by the audience, acts as a deterrent against too many departures from straight thinking.

In between the two extremes—the reasoning which is sincerely designed to discover truth, and that which is unashamedly designed to persuade—lies a large proportion of our thinking in which the motives are mixed.

PROPAGANDA AND ADVERTISING

Those who write political propaganda would admit that they are trying to persuade, but what they are trying to persuade people to think is what they themselves believe to be true, and they would say that they have come to believe it true by exercising their reason in an unbiased search for truth. They would probably agree that like the debaters they tend rather to gloss over arguments and facts that may be favourable to the other side; but members of the general public, it would be said, are not very intelligent, they must have their attention called to the truth, it must be emphasized and stressed; there is no point in calling attention to the items on that side of the scales which is outweighed. The vital point for the public interest and the good of the community is that the 'right' side should be successful in the election and a too scrupulous regard to valid reasoning, clear, unemotional thinking, might not serve this end.

The advertiser again is quite frankly trying to persuade. He will be careful not to make claims that can be nailed as untrue for, quite apart from any ethical considerations, he would find himself in trouble if he did. But there are quite often statements which appear in advertisements whose implications are to say the least of it misleading, and it is perhaps not being unduly cynical to suppose that the advertisers realize this. They would probably admit that they are interested not so much in the pursuit of truth as in extending the sales of various commodities. It is interesting that their appeal is very often to prestige; sometimes by implication, when the well-dressed important people are seen smoking —— cigarettes or drinking —— whisky, and sometimes openly, 'Top people read the . . .'. It may well be argued that to make such an appeal is to provide a perfectly valid reason why the customers should buy their goods; a great many of us would like our prestige to be enhanced, to be considered as of the 'Top people', and it is unfortunately true that such prestige does sometimes to some extent depend on the material goods we wear or use, though not nearly as much as the advertisers would have us believe.

All this is not at all to imply that there is necessarily anything wrong in trying to persuade people. It obviously depends what it is about which we are trying to persuade them. But if we are the objects of persuasion, of political propaganda, of advertising, or of some other form, we do well to realize what the purpose of the exercise is, to scrutinize the facts and the reasoning carefully and to see appeals to prestige and emotion for what they are.

PART PLAYED BY EMOTION

Most of us, if we examine our own private thinking or our methods of carrying on an argument, will have to admit that a disinterested desire to find out the truth is not always our sole or main motive. Or perhaps it would be better to say that the desire for truth which is acting as a motive is not entirely disinterested, that we genuinely desire to know the truth provided that it turns out to be what we want it to be. How often in our thinking we start from a conclusion, which has been dictated by emotion, prejudice or habit, and then look round for the reasons, the arguments which will support this conclusion, at the same time turning a convenient blind eye to those that don't. People will often for example support a political party from habit, because their parents have always voted that way, because it is unusual and not very respectable among the people with whom they mix to support any other party. But it is not very often that these will be admitted as the reasons, people are more likely to produce what would be generally regarded as more 'rational' arguments, that is arguments based on thinking and not on feeling.

Again it is quite likely that a man will support a political party because he thinks that the policies of that party with regard, say, to Income Tax, Super Tax, Nationalization, are more likely to react to his own interest than the policies of any other party. There is clearly nothing in the least irrational about this; the propaganda of the party will have been designed to persuade him (and other members of the electorate) of just that very fact, that their policies would be in his interests. Such a man, if he thinks excessively of such motives, may be accused of being selfish but not of being irrational. The latter accusation could only be brought against him if he pretends that his motives are different, if, having decided that he will vote for a party because he thinks that if they get in he will become a richer man, he then produces another more 'respectable' reason and perhaps almost persuades himself that that is the true one.

It is important to remember that in a great deal of our reasoning which is about open systems our emotions may be an essential part of the data, what we want is very far from being irrelevant. Our thinking should not be 'wishful' in the sense that we think a thing is so because we want it to be so, but it is certainly right, and indeed inevitable that the ends at which we aim should be dictated by our desires. That is what Hume meant when he said 'Reason is and ought only to be the slave of the passions', a dictum which is capable of being wrongly interpreted as expressing approval for the passions (especially the baser ones) and disapproval of the reasoning powers. In fact it merely states what is obvious, that men individually and collectively try to get what they want (food, drink, a higher standard of living for themselves and for others, culture, music, heaven on earth or heaven hereafter) and use their reason to devise means for these ends.

What is vital is that we should be clear-sighted and honest about this, that we should see and understand the role that the emotions play and accept them as an essential part of the data of many of the problems which the reason is set to solve.

It is important that we should be able to recognize the factors, habit, sentiment and prejudice, that influence our thinking. It is also important that we should try to preserve in discussion the ability to set out fairly what our conclusions are and why, and the flexibility to be prepared to change our minds if the weight of evidence and arguments is such as to persuade us that that is a reasonable thing to do. Most of us dislike admitting that we were wrong and have at least a slight obstinate disinclination to relinquish a view that we have strongly held in the past, whatever the evidence may be now. At the same time it is certainly not desirable to flit too easily from opinion to opinion swayed by whatever views one has heard most recently and most forcefully expressed. The second extreme—of excessive willingness to alter opinions—seems on the whole to be a less common failing than that of excessive unwillingness. When even intelligent people are discussing controversial matters they are often trying to win an argument instead of patiently, open-mindedly trying to acquire knowledge from the opinions and arguments put forward by other people, and contributing to the knowledge of others in the same way.

It is not perhaps possible that all disputation should be completely logically valid. As we have seen the verbal weapons that are used are not always capable of sufficient accuracy to make this so. It is certainly not either possible or desirable that disputation should not sometimes be persuasive or founded on sentiment or emotion. And life would be a trifle colourless if arguments were never overstated. But it is highly desirable that we should be able to recognize whether, to what extent, and in what ways this is so. And we should be able to distinguish between opinions that are reasonably based on sentiment and those that are unreasonably so based. If someone approves of fox-hunting because he regards those who don't as a lot of long-haired intellectuals with whom he doesn't wish to be associated, that would be generally regarded as an opinion that is irrationally based, whereas if someone approves of it because he enjoys it, that is a rational basis though some people would argue that it was an inadequate one.

SOME ERRORS ENUMERATED

In order that we may more easily be able to detect in our own thinking and that of others the sort of mistakes which we have been describing in general terms, we shall attempt now an enumeration of some of the more important ones. In many cases mention has already been made of them in earlier chapters. It is not very easy to draw a clear line between mistakes that might be described as purely logical, and therefore more likely to be genuine mistakes, and those that might be described as tricks of deception, in reasoning where the object is to persuade. On the whole I have tried to start with the logical mistakes and move on towards the deceptive tricks. This list makes no claim to be exhaustive.

(1) The verbal fallacy, i.e. the use of the same word in different senses in the course of the same piece of reasoning. We have seen some examples of this in an earlier chapter. It is a fruitful source of error and is most likely to mislead or deceive when the senses in which the word is used differ from each other only slightly.

(2) 'Undistributed' middle. This was mentioned specifically in the chapter on 'Syllogisms'. From the facts that 'some A's are B's' and 'some A's are C's' it is not legitimate to infer any connection between B's and C's: the middle term (the A's) is 'undistributed' (i.e. reference is made to only part of the class not to all of it) in both its appearances. From the facts that some Frenchmen live in London and some Frenchmen eat frogs we cannot derive any information as to whether some Londoners eat frogs.

(3) Excluded middle. This is the assumption in reasoning or questioning that one of two extreme positions must be true, thereby excluding the possibility of a middle course. We have referred to the idea in an earlier chapter as the logic of Yes or No, Black or White. About some things the assumption will be true ('Either you did or did not catch the 7.15 from Paddington'); but about many it will not ('Either you like this picture or you don't').

It is an assumption that is sometimes unfairly made in cross-examination of a witness when he is asked to answer a question 'Yes or No'. And this same demand may also be unfairly made when the questioner demands that more than one question should be answered simultaneously by a single Yes or No, or when the question is framed in such a way as to assume something which is not true.

To ask someone 'Is it or is it not the case that the murder was brutal, premeditated, took place at 5.30 and was done with a pocket knife? Answer me Yes or No!' would clearly be unreasonable. (This is sometimes referred to in books on Logic as the Fallacy of Many Questions.)

Again many of us might resent the implication which the questioner seems to be making if we are asked 'Are you as good as ever at avoiding hard work?' and feel that we cannot answer it by a simple Yes or No.

(4) The application of a general principle to particular cases regardless of the special circumstances.

This is not on the whole a mistake that the scientists are likely to make, because they should be trained in such a way as to realize that their general principles are conditioned and dependent upon circumstances. It is a mistake that is far more likely to occur when generalizations are being made about abstract matters and in political affairs. Recently in this country Conservatives have accused Socialists of doing it about the general principle that the means of production and distribution should be nationalized; and Socialists have accused Conservatives of doing it with regard to the general principle that freedom from control in business and in other things is to be desired. Both sides have applied the same adjective 'doctrinaire' in a derogatory way to the principle of their opponents in adhering to a general principle of their political creed irrespective of particular circumstances.

(5) To suppose that we can argue thus:

'If *p*, then *q*: but *q*, therefore *p*.' We have seen that this argument is not valid either when we are considering logical premiss and conclusion in a closed system, or when we are considering cause and effect in an open system. If a number is divisible by 12 it is even, but the fact that a number is even does not entitle us to deduce that it is divisible by 12.

If I were a very rich man I would buy myself a new hat; but

the fact that I have bought myself a new hat doesn't necessarily imply that I have become a very rich man.

(6) To suppose that because B happens after A happens A must therefore have caused B. This is sometimes called the fallacy: '*Post hoc, ergo propter hoc.*'

This is the sort of mistake that is likely to be made when causes and effects are particularly complicated and difficult to trace, and it is obviously only likely to cause trouble, that is to be dangerous and misleading, when it is at least possible that A might have caused B.

If a Government imposes a tax on commodities in April with the declared intention of preventing prices and wages from rising, and in May prices and wages rise, the opponents of the Government will naturally say '*propter hoc*', in other words that their action caused this. Their supporters on the other hand will probably claim that wages and prices would have risen much more otherwise. About the only thing that could be said with certainty in such a situation is that any '*ergo propter hoc*' claim would have to be qualified and tentative.

(7) Begging the question. This is one of the very commonest sources of error.

It occurs when in thinking or in argument we tacitly assume the matter which is under discussion, the point that we are purporting to prove. At an elementary level this is usually fairly obvious. Suppose that someone who is claiming to prove that Katie is older than Tommy argues thus: 'I know that Barbara and Tommy are the same age and of course Barbara must be younger than Katie because Tommy is. So as Katie is older than Barbara she must be older than Tommy too.' It is quite clear here that in saying that Tommy is younger than Katie the question at issue is being assumed.

Or again consider this argument: 'Smith cannot have told you a lie when he said he was my cousin, for no cousin of mine would ever tell a lie.' No comment is necessary. In both these cases it might equally be said that the argument is proceeding in a circle. A is assumed in order to prove B and then B is used to prove A. The greater the number of intermediate steps and the more the whole process is wrapped up in verbiage the less easy will it be to detect the mistake.

The same fallacy may occur in a slightly veiled form with statements where there is some doubt as to whether they should be interpreted as being empirical or analytic.

Suppose I say: 'Jones can't be a Communist because Jones is quite a sensible chap and no Communists are sensible.'

The form of this argument is perfectly sound and if one accepts the premisses the conclusion must be true. But most of us would probably not feel very happy about it. There is a feeling that in the context the statement 'No Communists are sensible' is a question-begging device. If, as is probable, it is just a generalization derived from a certain number of instances it begs the question by assuming, what is the matter at issue, that this 'quite sensible chap' cannot be a Communist. The statement 'No Communists are sensible' might on the other hand be entirely analytic, meaning that the speaker declares his intention of not applying the label 'sensible' to anyone who is a Communist. In this case the conclusion would only follow in the sense that if Jones already has the 'sensible' label round his neck it must have been known that he was not a Communist. The third possibility is that the statement might be an authentic empirical statement. The criteria for being sensible having been decided on grounds other than that of being a Communist, an examination is made of all Communists and it is discovered that in no case do they satisfy the criteria for being sensible. The conclusion that Jones cannot be a Communist is therefore true, but it can hardly be said to 'follow' as that fact must have been part of the evidence for the generalization.

Whichever way one looks at it therefore there is a question-begging element about this argument. The sort of thought that is likely to have lain behind it might be expressed in a less extreme and more reasonable way thus:

'I should be surprised if Jones is a Communist. He seems a pretty sensible chap in other ways and I don't think that a Communist is a sensible thing to be.'

The illicit assumptions that we have considered so far have lain near the surface and have been easy to detect. If the question that is being begged is a simple fact, such as that Katie is older than Tommy, it is hardly possible that it should be wrapped up. In a more complicated argument, however, which is dealing with abstractions, in which the premisses and conclusions are less clear-cut, it is more likely that the begging or the partial begging of a question may be subtly concealed and difficult to detect. If a politician for example is arguing on rational grounds that a redistribution of wealth is to the public benefit it is very likely that somewhere in the course of his argument a flat statement to this effect, expressed perhaps more lengthily in other words, will be used as a premiss in his reasoning. This sort of thing is particularly likely to happen in philosophical arguments. Suppose for example that one is arguing as to which of two theories of truth is true—that is to say as to whether a statement has to satisfy criterion X or criterion Y in order to have a truth-label attached to it. Those who are in favour of criterion X will naturally tend to apply this in trying to decide whether it is the right criterion, whether it provides a true theory of truth; and similarly for those who are in favour of criterion Y. But to do this is to beg the question at issue.

When it occurs in a seriously misleading form, as it often does, this fallacy is based fundamentally on a lack of intellectual imagination, the inability to imagine a state of affairs which is other than what we in fact think it is. The arguer starts off with a great to-do about not having any preconceived notions, examining affairs with a clear unbiased mind, but suddenly somewhere in the argument the preconceived notion appears and no one is more genuinely unaware of its appearance or deceived by the argument founded on it than its innocent possessor. In its complex and dangerous form this is not usually a matter of deliberate deception. This lack of imagination is well exemplified by the old lady who was so glad that she didn't like cabbages because if she did she would eat such a lot of them and she did dislike them so.

We should be particularly on the look-out for examples of this mistake in our own thinking as well as in that of other people.

(8) Argument by Analogy. This is, as we have seen already, an argument by the consideration of similar cases. The trouble is that they may be taken to be more similar than they really are.

The pointing out of similarities may be useful and interesting and may serve to illustrate points and draw attention to, and emphasize, important and helpful ways of looking at the matter. But analogies can never be validly used to establish conclusions although they may sometimes point to them.

It is perhaps worth pointing out the difference between a metaphor and an analogy. If I say Smith has an eye like a hawk or a heart of gold I am speaking metaphorically. In the first example I am pointing out a similarity between Smith and a hawk —namely that they both have very good eyesight. Our language abounds with phrases of this type—brave as a lion, fit as a fiddle, flat as a pancake, straight as an arrow—which are used so often that they have become clichés, that is to say they are used without reflection and no longer serve the purpose, as they no doubt did when they were first coined, of vividly illustrating or illuminating the bravery, the fitness, the flatness, or whatever it was that was being talked about. As Susan Stebbing has pointed out they are metaphors which might be described, metaphorically, as dead or at least as half-dead. In many cases the point of the metaphor, the similarity to which attention is being called, is now rather obscure. Why fit as a fiddle? And what is the merit of having a heart of gold?

It is when the metaphor is taken a stage further, that is when from similarities of one kind a similarity of another kind is inferred, that we get an Analogy. Suppose I say: 'The razor edge of his intellect will be blunted by constant use.' A man's brain-power is here being compared to a razor or to anything that has a sharp edge. The metaphor is a useful one and may illustrate vividly how really intelligent people seem to be able to cut (metaphorically) through a mass of complications and go straight to the (metaphorical) heart of a problem. But the implication of the statement seems to be that just as a razor will be blunted by constant use so will a man be able to think less effectively if he thinks a lot. This is therefore an analogy.

It would probably be agreed that it is not a very good one. Most people find that by thinking a lot their minds are rendered more efficient (i.e. sharper) and not less so. It is true of course that one may get tired from overwork, but on the whole the efficiency of a man's intellect is not very similar to the sharpness of a razor: the latter deteriorates steadily from a maximum starting point, the former is, at least up to a point, improved by use. Even if the analogy were a good one it would provide no argument: the intellect would not be blunted by use *because* it was like a razor, but it would be like a razor because it was blunted by use.

Consider another example:

'Crabnuff's action has thrown a spanner into the works of the machinery of negotiation. So complex is this machinery that it may take many months to repair.'

If it is known from a consideration of the factors involved that as a result of Crabnuff's action it may be many months before negotiations can be resumed this would be a perfectly harmless metaphor. But it might be designed to persuade people that just as when spanners are thrown into complicated pieces of machinery they may take months to repair (are there no spare parts?), so in this case with the machinery of negotiation; and the 'just as ... so ...' might be used nearly in the sense of 'because ... therefore ...'. In this case it would be an illegitimate argument by analogy.

Metaphors leading to analogies are very common in political arguments. One of the commonest and the most dangerous concerns the 'body politic'. The State (or any association) is compared to a human being, the Government or ruling authority is as the mind, and various organs of the state may be compared to various limbs or organs of the body. This may in certain contexts be a vivid and useful metaphor. But when it forms the basis of an argument by analogy it may be seriously misleading. Consider, for example, the following extract from Bacon:

> No body can be healthful without exercise, neither natural body nor politic; and, certainly, to a kingdom, or estate, a just and honourable war is the true exercise. A civil war, indeed, is like the heat of a fever; but a foreign war is like the heat of exercise, and serveth to keep the body in health; for in a slothful peace, both courages will effeminate and manners corrupt.

The argument is quite clear: exercise is good for the human body; what corresponds to exercise for the body politic is a foreign war; therefore a foreign war is good for the body politic.

The similarity between the natural body and the body politic is assumed.

This argument would be much less likely now than when it was written to persuade people of the desirability of a foreign war. We have come to be convinced by less theoretical considerations that it is not healthful for the body politic. We may infer from this that there is little similarity between war for a nation and exercise for an individual, or that there is little similarity between the natural body and the body politic, or both. But again, even if these two 'bodies' were much more alike than we now think them to be, however close was the parallel between war for a nation and exercise for an individual, the conclusion that war was healthful for the nation as exercise was for the individual would not at all follow, but would have to be established on separate grounds.

In fact the fallacy of 'Argument by Analogy' is that it is *never* possible to argue by analogy. A and B may be similar in seventeen different ways and these similarities may be observed, commented on and form the basis of interesting metaphors, but we can never go on to argue that because A has some other property 'x', therefore B has it too. We can perhaps argue that the fact that they are similar in so many ways makes it likely that other similarities exist too, but if we examine cases where we use metaphor and analogy we see that even this is hardly justifiable. The whole point of metaphor and analogy is that the things compared are basically dissimilar. 'Brave as a lion', is a metaphor, but 'Brave as Mr. Jones' is not (unless it is applied to lions). An analogy may be drawn between a nation and a ship ('The Ship of State') but these are obviously dissimilar in very many more aspects than they are similar. If we compare the nation that is Great Britain with France this would not be an analogy because they are basically similar.

In fact, then, analogies may be useful in illustrating points and helping us to understand complicated ideas, and they are often used for this purpose by scientists. But they can never be used to establish a conclusion.

(9) Misrepresentations. We come now to a whole class of errors and deceptions in argument which it would be difficult and perhaps rather tedious to enumerate in detail, and which can be roughly covered by the single title 'Misrepresentations'.

This misrepresentation may be due to stupidity or to dishonesty, it may be of one's own case or of one's opponent's. Attempts may be made to bolster up one's own case by irrelevant considerations. These may take the form of an appeal to prestige or a claim to inside information and superior knowledge; there are many occasions of course where such an appeal and such a claim may be perfectly justifiable and relevant, but there are also many occasions on which they are used when they are not. There is also an appeal to emotion. This again may not be irrelevant but its introduction is in fact a device which is often used to cloud the issue.

One may misrepresent one's case by over-emphasis or re-peated assertion, though this is quite likely to have an effect which is the reverse of that intended. One may prove a conclu-sion which is slightly and subtly different from that which one is claiming to prove.

The larger class of misrepresentations, however, is concerned with one's opponent and his case. One such trick is well known under its Latin name: '*Argumentum ad hominem*'. It consists of attacking the man instead of what he is arguing about. In the witness-box, where this method is used to cast doubt on the general reliability of a witness, it may not be irrelevant but it is not often justifiable in a rational discussion. The attack on the man may take many forms: pointing out that he was wrong last week, attempting to puncture his prestige, or casting reflections on his intelligence either by the direct method ('I should have thought it was fairly obvious that...') or by the inverse, in-direct method ('Of course I'm a mere simpleton in these matters...').

The misrepresentation of one's opponent's case may take the form of just a plain mis-statement of it, or, more subtly, the form of attacking a slightly different position, perhaps a more extreme one, from that which is being defended. Or one may attack the case by casting doubt on the reliability or sufficiency of the evidence produced. This is a perfectly reasonable and legitimate thing to do but if it is followed up, as it often is, by those who are beginning to see that their case is exceedingly weak, by the assertion that as we can't know all the facts we had better suspend judgement, one is justified in feeling suspicious. We very seldom do know all the relevant facts but we may yet be justified in forming an opinion on the basis of what is known, and a plea for the suspension of judgement is likely to come from someone who recognizes that the facts which are available indicate a conclusion which is unpalatable to him.

Another device of controversy, which is used more by those who are trying to persuade people to do something than by those who are trying to win an argument in the ordinary sense, is that of attacking vigorously and lengthily a position that is known to be impregnable, and then suddenly stopping and conceding the point. The opposition is likely to relax, relieved and triumphant, and other positions may be captured with ease, other concessions had for the asking. This is a device which the young often learn to use against authority when they ask for more than they can possibly expect to get, and eventually emerge with a 'compromise' which they would never have obtained if they had restricted their original request to it.

AN EXAMPLE CONSIDERED

We will now examine and discuss a passage from Plato:

(1) 'Then let us put it this way,' I said. 'The just man does not compete with his like, but only his unlike, while the unjust man competes with both like and unlike.'

'That puts it very well.'

'And the unjust man is a man of good sense, the just man not?'

'Well said again.'

'And so the unjust man is like the man of good sense, while the just man is not?'

M

'Of course he must *be like* what he *is*, and the just man unlike.'

'Good. So each of them resembles what he is like.'

'Well, what next?'

'So far, so good, Thrasymachus. Do you recognize the distinction between being musical and unmusical?'

'Yes.'

'And which of the two involves knowledge?'

'Being musical; and being unmusical does not.'

'And knowledge is good, ignorance bad.'

'Yes.'

'And the same argument applies to medicine.'

'It does.'

'Then does one musician who is tuning a lyre try to compete with another, or think that he ought to improve on the correct tuning of the instrument?'

'I think not.'

'But he does try to do better than an unmusical layman?'

'He must try to do that.'

'What about a doctor then? Does he want to go beyond what is correct in his prescriptions in competition with his fellow-doctors?'

'No.'

'But he tries to do better than the layman?'

'Yes.'

'Then do you think that over the whole range of professional skill, anyone who has such skill aims at anything more in word or deed than anyone with similar skill? Don't they both aim at the same result in similar circumstances?'

'I suppose there's no denying that.'

'But the man who has no skill will try to compete both with the man who has and with the man who has not.'

'Maybe.'

'And the man with professional knowledge is wise and the wise man is good.'

'I agree.'

'So the good man, who has knowledge, will not try to compete with his like, but only with his opposite.'

'So it seems.'

'While the bad and ignorant man will try to compete both with his like and with his opposite.'

'So it appears.'

'But it was surely the unjust man, Thrasymachus, who, we found, competes both with his like and his unlike? That was what you said, wasn't it?'

'It was,' he admitted.

'While the just man will not compete with his like, but with his unlike.'

'True.'

'The just man, then,' I said, 'resembles the good man who has knowledge, the unjust the man who is ignorant and bad.'

'That may be.'

'But we agreed that a thing *is* what it is *like*.'

'We did.'

'Then,' I concluded, 'we have shown that the just man is wise and good and the unjust bad and ignorant.'

> (Plato's *Republic*, translation by H. D. P. Lee, Penguin, pp. 79–81)

We need not be concerned here to question the assumptions from which this argument starts, or the conclusions to which it leads, but only to consider whether, granted these assumptions, the argument is valid.

Let us summarize:

'The just man competes with his unlike only and is not a man of good sense. The unjust man competes with both like and unlike and is a man of good sense. Expert doctors and musicians compete with their unlike only, while those who are inexpert compete with like and unlike.

Therefore the just man resembles the expert Doctor and Musician.

But the expert Doctor or Musician is wise and good.

And "we agreed that a thing *is* what it is *like*".

Therefore the just man is wise and good.'

The most obvious fallacy here is the assumption that because A and B have one characteristic in common therefore they have others. This is like saying that because Smith and Jones both wear trousers and Smith is kind to animals therefore Jones is kind to animals too. If this argument were to be used it could equally well, on the assumptions of the above passage, lead to the conclusion that the expert Doctor and Musician are unjust, for they have been stated to be wise and good or 'men of good sense' and we start from the assumption that the unjust man is a 'man of good sense'.

Notice also the illegitimate inversion from 'of course he must be like what he is', early in the passage, to 'we agreed that a thing *is* what it is *like*', later.

Examples on Chapter 9

1. Comment on the following:

(i) There is nothing surprising or even particularly regrettable in the fact that the economy has recently been slowing down, that production has not been increasing. After all, even the best of batsmen plays a maiden over occasionally; you can't expect anyone to score sixes and fours all the time.

(ii) Heard in court:

'If you hadn't been there the accident wouldn't have happened.'

'No, of course not.'

'So you admit it was your fault.'

(iii) 'The Coroner, in his summing up, said that Mr. —— elected to dip his lights as a car approached from the opposite direction. "I am always against the dipping of lights unless the driver of the approaching car dips his. Had Mr. —— not dipped his lights he would have seen these girls".'

(From a *Times* report)

(iv) 'In civilized society, personal merit will not serve you so much as money will. Sir, you may make the experiment. Go into the street and give one man a lecture on morality, and another a shilling, and see which will respect you most.'

(Dr. Johnson, as reported by Boswell)

(v) It is the clear duty of the Press to publish such news as it shall be in the public interest to have published. There can be no doubt about the public interest taken in the brutal murder of —— and the private life of ——. The Press would therefore have been failing in their duty if they had refrained from publishing the details of these things.

(vi) 'Mr. Butler could help the economy by eliminating all Ministries that did not exist before the war. The country ran without them then, and can do so now.'

(Letter to *Daily Express*)

(vii) 'To the British, who have always regarded the French as pre-eminently a logical people, it has seemed strange that France should have adopted so empirical an approach to her colonial policies.'

(*The Times*, 19 August, 1958)

(viii) The modification of the past as quickly as possible to meet the circumstances of the future is the one policy which is going to bring us as a Government and as a nation up, up, and up, and on, on, and on. . . .

(Ramsay MacDonald)

(ix) 'I fail to see why hunting should be so desperately cruel when it gives a tremendous lot of employment to a lot of people, and a lot of pleasure.'

(x) 'Sir,

The Rev. —— in his letter today, questions the validity of the speculation by biographers about the character of their subject when based on a portrait which is a "no-portrait". Apparently, like most people, he assumes that in the living person "the thin lips, the sensitive nostril, the bewildered look in the eye, and so on" do indicate certain characteristics. But is there, Sir, any scientific or factual basis for this widely held assumption?

Yours faithfully'

(Letter to *The Times*)

(xi) It's not much good your going to the wicket and scoring sometimes a single, sometimes a four or a six, and sometimes no runs at all for six consecutive balls. How do you think a manufacturer would survive if on some days he produced no goods, some days half a dozen and on other days larger amounts? Steady, consistent, preferably consistently increasing production should be the target for the cricketer as for the businessman.

(xii) Many Socialist intellectuals consider it 'de rigueur' to find the proletariat superior to other people, while professing a desire to abolish the conditions which, according to them, alone produce good human beings.

(xiii) 'Science is said to enable "man to conquer nature". As a roundabout way of saying that scientific knowledge helps men to become wealthier and healthier, it may pass. Provided health and wealth are used as means to good ends, it is matter for self-congratulation, but otherwise, not. However, the phrase contains a double confusion: first, because on any proper interpretation men are themselves part of nature; secondly, because the only conquest a man can achieve is over other men, by compelling them to do his will. The instruments provided by science have indeed made this kind of conquest far more dangerous—hardly matter for congratulation.'

(A. D. Ritchie, *Civilization, Science and Religion*)

2. Discuss whether the metaphors used in the following passages are apt, and whether they illuminate and enforce the points that are being made:

(i) 'The Public Accounts Committee of the House of Commons is rightly respected inside and outside Parliament, but its report published yesterday illustrated a weakness in its working that is recognized in the House of Commons but not always understood outside.

'The committee is essentially a blunt instrument—a bludgeon rather than a rapier. Surveying as it does the accounts of all the departments, its criticisms can rarely be founded on a profound study of any one subject....'

(Letter to *The Times*)

(ii) 'If the transfer of energy from Religion to Economics at the opening of the Modern Age of Western history had shot a bolt that had subsequently come home to roost like a boomerang in the economic field, it was conceivable that a re-transfer of energy from Economics to Religion at the opening of a post-Modern age might ultimately come to a self-stultified Western Homo Economicus's rescue.'

(A. J. Toynbee, *A Study of History*, IX, 641)

3. Boswell 'wishes to have it settled whether duelling is contrary to the laws of Christianity'.

Dr. Johnson says: 'Sir, as men become in a high degree refined, various causes of offence arise; which are considered to be of such importance, that life must be staked to atone for them, though in reality they are not so. A body that has received a very fine polish may be easily hurt. Before men arrive at this artificial refinement, if one tells his neighbour he lies, his neighbour tells him he lies; if one gives his neighbour a blow, his neighbour gives him a blow: but in a state of highly polished society, an affront is held to be a serious injury. It must therefore be resented, or rather a duel must be fought upon it, as men have agreed to banish from their society one who puts up with an affront without fighting a duel. Now, Sir, it is never unlawful to fight in self-defence. He, then, who fights a duel, does not fight from passion against his antagonist, but out of self-defence; to avert the stigma of the world, and to prevent himself from being driven out of society. I could wish there was not that superfluity of refinement; but while such notions prevail, no doubt a man may lawfully fight a duel.'

Summarize Dr. Johnson's argument and discuss its validity.

4. Discuss:

'Every species is vague, every term goes cloudy at its edges, and so in my way of thinking, relentless logic is only another phrase for a stupidity—for a sort of intellectual pigheadedness.'

(H. G. Wells)

5. Analyse the arguments contained in the following passages and discuss their validity:

(i) *'Buses are stung*

'Consider what high taxation does to the bus driver in particular. A chauffeur driving a black limousine for a nationalized board draws a wage of £7 10s. for a 43-hour week. He has charge of the safety of perhaps two passengers.

'The driver of a big red double-decker has charge of the safety of up to 60 passengers. Yet he draws a wage of £7 18s. 6d. for a 44-hour week.

'How does it come about that the bus driver receives so small an extra reward for so large an extra responsibility? One reason is that the buses must bear a tax of 2s. 6d. on every gallon of fuel that goes into the tank. That is a tax of 214 per cent!'

(*Daily Express*, 15 October, 1954)

(ii) 'Sir,

Dr. Huxley ridicules people who "still maintain that the planets are kept in their course by God and not by gravitation". He could equally ridicule those who maintained that London was lit by man and not by electricity.'

(Letter to the *Sunday Times*)

(iii) 'To say freedom makes possible experiment and discovery would justify the constraint of those whose use of their freedom involves no discoveries.'

(J. D. Mabbott, *The State and the Citizen*)

(iv) '—— was the great war-time pilot of this country, and if he was a good war-time pilot he is bound to be a good peace-time one.'

(v) 'Education implies teaching. Teaching implies knowledge. Knowledge is truth. The truth is everywhere the same. Hence education should be everywhere the same.'

(R. M. Hutchins, *The Higher Learning in America*)

6. Summarize and where necessary criticize the arguments of the following passages:

(i) 'In boxing and other kinds of fighting, skill in attack goes with skill in defence, does it not?'

'Of course.'

'So, too, the ability to save from disease implies the ability to produce it undetected, while ability to bring an army safely through a campaign goes with ability to rob the enemy of his secrets and steal a march on him in action.'

'I certainly think so.'

'So a man who's good at keeping a thing will be good at stealing it.'

'I suppose so.'

'So if the just man is good at keeping money safe he will be good at stealing it too.'

'That at any rate is the conclusion the argument leads to.'

'So the just man turns out to be a kind of thief.'

(Plato, *The Republic*, tr. by H. D. P. Lee)

(ii) '... we may perhaps take it as having been already demonstrated that an historian's professed inability to discern in History any plot, rhythm, or predetermined pattern is no evidence that blind Samson has actually won his boasted freedom from the bondage of "Laws of Nature". The presumption is, indeed, the opposite; for, when bonds are imperceptible to the wearer of them, they are likely to prove more difficult to shake off than when they betray their presence and reveal something of their shape and texture by clanking and galling.'

(A. J. Toynbee, *A Study of History*, IX, 196)

(iii) 'Good,' said I. 'And has not everything which has a function its own particular virtue or excellence? Let me take the same examples again. The eyes have a function; have they not also their own particular excellence?'

'They have.'

'The ears too have a function, and therefore their own excellence. And so with all other things?'

'Yes, that is so.'

'Come, then; could the eyes properly perform their function if instead of their own peculiar virtue or excellence they had the corresponding defect?'

'How could they? For you mean, I suppose, blindness instead of sight?'

'I mean whatever their virtue may be. For I am not concerned with that yet, but only to find out whether a thing's characteristic virtue enables it to perform its function well, while its characteristic defect makes it perform it badly.'

'Yes, that is true certainly,' he replied.

'So we can say that the ears if deprived of their own peculiar virtue perform their function badly; and the same argument applies in all other cases.'

'I agree.'

'Then the next point is this. Is there any function that it is impossible to perform except with the mind? For example, paying attention, controlling, deliberating and so on: can we divorce any of these from the conscious mind of which we should say they were characteristic?'

'No.'

'And life—is not that a function of mind?'

'Certainly.'

'And the mind therefore will have its peculiar virtue.'

'It will.'

'And if deprived of its peculiar virtue it will be incapable of performing its function well, will it not?'

'Quite incapable.'

'It follows therefore that goodness enables the mind to perform its functions of control and attention well, and badness the reverse.'

'It follows.'

'And we agreed, did we not, that justice was the peculiar virtue of the mind and injustice its defect?'

'We did.'

'So the just-minded man will have a good life, and the unjust a bad life?'

'So it appears from your argument.'

'But the man who has a good life is prosperous and happy, and his opposite the reverse?'

'Of course.'

'So the just man is happy, and the unjust man miserable?'

'I grant that.'

'And so, since it never pays to be miserable, but to be happy, we can say, my dear Thrasymachus, that justice pays better than injustice.'

(Plato, *The Republic*, tr. by H. D. P. Lee)

(iv) It will be generally agreed that the most virulent and dangerous disease of this decade is that of Inflation. The inflation of a balloon is caused by the injection of air; the inflation of an economy is caused by the injection of money. If a balloon is over-inflated it bursts—it no longer exists, and the air which supports it is mingled with the surrounding atmosphere. If an economy is over-inflated therefore, it too will burst, and the money which supported it in its prime will be scattered to the four winds of heaven.

Just as the cause of the bursting of a balloon is too much air too quickly, so the cause of economic inflation is uniquely and simply too much money, too soon, too quickly. The effects of inflation however are more complex and varied, and there may even be differences of opinion about them. There is a school of thought which inclines to the opinion that the effect of inflation is that the economy produces more; there is another school which is of the opinion that the effect is that the economy produces less. This apparent dilemma may be resolved by a very simple logical argument, which not merely unravels a tangled skein, but also demonstrates conclusively how potent a weapon theoretical argument can be in the hands of one who has been trained in its use.

The immediate effect of inflation must either be that prices rise or that prices fall. Suppose the former. If prices rise, more money is paid out, if more money is paid out more money must be injected into the balloon which is the economy. But this is inflation. We are led therefore by an inescapable logical process to the conclusion that inflation causes itself. It is a well-known principle however, both of logic and of life, that no event or entity can be its own cause. Our argument therefore is a *Reductio ad Absurdum*, and our supposition that inflation causes prices to rise must be erroneous. Inflation therefore causes prices to fall.

But just as what goes up must come down, so what goes down must previously have gone up. Prices in the past therefore must previously have risen; the economy must therefore have been producing more, and so as a result of inflation in the balloon economic it must now be producing less.

This argument will, I hope, expose once and for all the fallacies that must be contained in the figures produced by the Consoclibists purporting to show that the economy has in fact produced more. Everyone knows that we are suffering from inflation, and we have shown that this means lower production.

(v) 'Now although Baumann bases the concept of one on inner intuition, he refers nevertheless, in the passage just cited, to certain criteria for being one, namely being undivided and being isolated. If this were correct, then we should have to expect animals, too, to be capable of having some sort of idea of unity. Can it be that a dog staring at the moon does have an idea, however ill-defined, of what we signify by the word "one"? This is hardly credible—and yet it certainly distinguishes individual objects: another dog, its master, a stone it is playing with, these certainly appear to the dog every bit as isolated, as self-contained, as undivided, as they do to us. It will notice a difference, no doubt, between being set on by several other dogs and being set on by only one, but this is what Mill calls the physical difference. We need to know specifically: is the dog conscious, however dimly, of that common element in the two situations which we express by the word "one", when, for example, it first is bitten by one larger dog and then chases one cat? This seems to me unlikely. I infer, therefore, that the notion of unity is not, as Locke holds, "suggested to the understanding by every object without us, and every idea within", but becomes known to us through the exercise of those higher intellectual powers which distinguish men from brutes. Consequently, such properties of things as being undivided or being isolated, which animals perceive quite as well as we do, cannot be what is essential in our concept.'

(G. Frege, *The Foundations of Arithmetic*
translated by J. L. Austin)

(vi) I cannot forbear to add the following argument against Materialism which emanates from Professor Broad, partly because it affords so admirable an example of the logician's art, partly because it shows how formidable a weapon logic can be, when it is used to demolish the arguments of those who have paid more attention to science than to straight thinking. The argument is as follows: 'However completely the behaviour of the external body answers to the behaviouristic tests for intelligence, it always remains a perfectly sensible question to ask: "Has it really got a mind or is it merely an automaton?" It is quite true that we have no available means of answering such questions conclusively. It is also true that the more nearly a body answers to the behaviouristic tests for intelligence, the harder it is for us in practice to contemplate the possibility of its having no mind. Still the question "Has it a mind?" is never silly in the sense that it is meaningless. At worst, it is silly only in the sense that it does not generally express a real doubt, and that we have no means of answering it. It may be like asking whether the moon may not be made of green cheese; but it is not like asking whether a rich man may have no wealth. Now on the behaviouristic theory to have a mind means just to behave in certain ways, and to ask whether a thing which admittedly does behave in these ways has a mind would be like asking whether Jones, who is admittedly a rich man, has much wealth. Since the question can be raised, and is evidently not tautologous or self-contradictory, it is clear that when we ascribe a mind or a mental process to an external body, we do not mean simply that it behaves in certain characteristic'ways.'

(C. E. M. Joad)

7. Is the conclusion of the following proposition true? Discuss the argument.

Proposition XXXVII
A being cannot be the ultimate cause which terminates its own existence.

For, if any being can be the ultimate cause of terminating its own existence, it will act in the immediate antecedent points to, and the last point of duration that terminates its existence, in opposition to that power that continues it in its existence; and consequently will act in the point of duration that terminates its existence, in opposition to that power that continues it in its existence, so as to destroy its effect, which is absurd.

Therefore a being cannot be the ultimate cause which terminates its own existence; which was to be demonstrated.

(Richard Jack, *Mathematical Principles of Theology, or The Existence of God Geometrically Demonstrated*, 1747)

8. In his *Study of History* (Vol. IX, p. 195) Professor Arnold Toynbee quotes from H. A. L. Fisher as follows: 'One intellectual excitement has . . . been denied me. Men wiser and more learned than I have discerned in History a plot, a rhythm, a pre-determined pattern. These harmonies are concealed from me. I can see only one emergency following upon another as wave follows upon wave; only one great fact with respect to which, since it is unique, there can be no generaliza-

tions; only one safe rule for the historian: that he should recognize in the development of human destinies the play of the contingent and the unforeseen.'

Toynbee then goes on to comment: 'This declaration had become a "locus classicus" within seventeen years of the date of its publication; yet, before it was published, it had already been put out of court by its author's choice of his title for the book in which this prefatory passage was intended to strike the key-note. An historian who had thus publicly declared his allegiance to the dogma that "Life is just one damned thing after another" might have been expected to give his work some such conformably non-committal title as "A History of Some Emergencies in Some Human Affairs"; but in calling it, as he did, "A History of Europe", he was recanting in his title his own denial in his preface that he had "discerned in History a plot, a rhythm, a pre-determined pattern"; for the portmanteau word "Europe" is a whole "Corpus Juris Naturae" in itself.'

Discuss the logic of Professor Toynbee's criticism.

10

Solving Problems

ALL that has been written in this book is designed to help the reader to think more clearly by studying the logical connections of premisses and conclusions, and the practical connections of causes and effects. In the last chapter we tried to show how the lessons learnt enabled us to analyse more critically the thoughts and arguments of other people, and to detect accidental mistakes and deliberate deceptions in their reasoning.

We come now to the consideration of that to which every-thing that has gone before is merely a means, to the process which is what thinking of every kind is ultimately for, the solution of problems.

THE CLASSIFICATION OF PROBLEMS

We use the word 'problem' here in a very wide sense. In prac-tice it is often reserved for what we should call a difficult problem ('That can be solved very easily, there's no problem there'), but we are taking it for the moment to cover any situation where we ask *how* something is to be done, what is to be done next, what is the answer to this question (where it is not simply a matter of memory, fact or opinion): in fact any situation where thinking is required. There is an inevitable circularity in saying that the ob-ject of all our thinking is to solve problems and then going on to define problems as anything for which thinking is required. This is a case where enumeration is better than definition, or denota-tion than connotation.

How to get to Liverpool before midnight, what is 83 times

792, how to make my car go, how to checkmate Black in two moves, who murdered Bloggs the Butler, how to cross the road without getting run over, how to find the square root of 7,891, how to cure Inflation, what has caused the recent increase in juvenile delinquency: these are all problems, but they are clearly of very different kinds and of very different degrees of difficulty.

One broad and useful distinction that can be made is between problems that arise from what we have called 'closed' systems of thinking and those that arise from 'open' systems. Most mathematical problems, all thinking over the chess board, the questions of formal logic—for example which of the 256 syllogisms are valid ones—are in the first category, and all practical problems, the questions of applied science, the day-to-day problems of life, and the perennial problem of how to make the world a better place, are in the second. The distinction is not completely clear-cut; there are many problems about which we might argue as to which category they belong to, and many which, it might be claimed, belong to both. Such arguments would not on the whole be profitable, but the distinction is useful because it brings out important differences in the nature of the questions asked and the nature of the solutions. The distinction is almost the same as one between theoretical and practical problems.

The closed systems are by definition artificial; the questions asked are usually quite clear and unambiguous ('What is the cube root of 729?', 'How can I avoid losing my bishop next move?'), and the solutions are much more likely to be cut-and-dried and definite. And they are likely to be more definite in two ways: in the first place there is likely to be a precise, correct answer, and in the second place it is likely to be known from the nature of the question or the way it is put whether there is such an answer. We usually know exactly what we are looking for, we usually know also whether it is there to be found, and there is not likely to be much difficulty in recognizing whether we have found it or not.

In an open system, however, it is mainly the easy problems which are clear and unambiguous and admit of a definite solution. ('What is the shortest way by road from A to B?', 'What caused that book to fall off the table?')

Many of the toughest problems are such that it may not always be known whether a solution is possible. When Economists and Politicians, for example, are trying to find a cure for Inflation they may not be entirely agreed as to what Inflation is, they are likely to be in doubt both as to whether a solution is possible and also as to what would count as a solution. The solution of an open system problem may often be rather like a search for a needle in a haystack which is handicapped, not only by its not being certain whether a needle is there, but also by the fact that the searchers are rather hazy as to whether they would recognize it if they found it.

The problems that arise in real life, in fact, are very often not such as to admit of a solution which is right or wrong. It is true that to most mathematical problems there is one right solution and an indefinitely large number of wrong ones, but it is not true that 'there is a right and a wrong way of doing everything'. There are better ways and there are ways which are not so good; there are steps which can be taken to alleviate the disadvantages of Inflation and it is desirable to go on searching for ways in which the situation can be improved still further. But it is wrong and misleading to think of the problem of Inflation as one to which there is a unique, correct solution which would instantly be recognized as such if only we could find it.

This is an extreme case where there is vagueness both as regards the question and the possibility of solution, but the same remarks apply to a lesser degree to a whole host of practical, open system problems. It is not a matter of finding *the* solution, it is a matter rather of finding a better method, of gradual improvement, of tentative suggestions, of experimental hypotheses. And if one

N

approaches this kind of problem with what one might call a 'closed-system' mind, expecting clear-cut solutions, the results are likely to be unfortunate.

A further difference that is worth noting between open-system and closed-system problems is that, on the whole, it is only in a closed-system that the same situation can repeat itself precisely. This is clearly because of the artificiality of the system and the fact that it is insulated from the real world of unpredictable events. The importance of this is simply to be warned against the danger of treating similar situations in an open system as though they were exactly the same. It is true that the scientist can very often in the laboratory introduce this artificiality, he can to a very considerable extent insulate his experiments from the unpredictability of the world of events, but the historian and the social scientist have got to be very careful to remember that in their departments no two situations are ever exactly the same, although they may closely resemble each other in a lot of significant and important ways.

APPLYING A RULE

We come now to consider some methods of solving problems of all sorts. The first and basic method that we use is that of applying a rule.

It is obvious that in its early stages a large part of our education consists in learning rules, learning how and when to apply them, and practising their application. When we are taking our first steps in Latin, for example, our success depends partly on our memory and partly on our ability to apply rules like: 'The object must always be in the accusative,' '*Ut* with final clauses is followed by the subjunctive.' In order to do this we must of course be able to recognize objects and final clauses and to know what the accusative and the subjunctive are.

Similarly, in the early stages of Mathematics, once we know

by heart the multiplication tables we go on to learn and to practise the application of rules such as those for long division and multiplication, finding a square root and so on. A difference here is that in Mathematics the reasons for the rule can be explained and the student persuaded that it is *right*, that it follows inevitably from the nature of numbers and the way we count. And it is generally regarded as a very important part of the task of the Mathematical teacher to undertake such explanation, to try to ensure that his pupils are capable of thinking things out for themselves, that they do not work merely by rule of thumb, by applying a succession of formulae. But although the Mathematician should be able to justify his rules if required, he will not normally think out the justification every time he uses them: once they have been mastered and understood it saves time and trouble to apply them automatically.

The rules in Latin, however, do not have the same inevitability about them, they might perfectly well have been different; the accusative of '*mensa*', the case into which the object is normally put, might have been '*mensae*' instead of '*mensam*'. To the enquirer who asks 'Why?' the only answer is: 'It just is; that is the rule, and the rule was based on the way in which the language was developed by those who used it.'

If these rules consist merely of one simple step they are obviously very easy to apply; also the more limited and narrow they are, in the sense of being unambiguously and closely defined, the less scope will there be for initiative and enterprise on the part of the person who is applying them, and the more likely it will be that they will be correctly applied. If one is asked to put a succession of sentences of the precise type: 'Balbus builds a wall' into Latin, then provided that a dictionary and grammar are available and the rule has been properly taught, there is not much possibility of error; there is no room for manoeuvre, as it were, no opportunity for an imaginative and different, and therefore incorrect, interpretation of the rule. Similarly a succession of long multiplication sums to anyone who has been taught the rule and knows his tables is almost entirely a test of care and accuracy.

As the student moves on to more advanced levels in these subjects however the rules become more complicated and therefore harder to apply. There will also, increasingly, be the difficulty of knowing which of the many rules that have been collected is the appropriate one. At the elementary stages the student is usually given a series of examples which provide him with the opportunity of practising the application of the rule he has just learned. He will know that the Latin sentences are all about '*quominus*' and '*quin*' or that the geometrical riders are all about the angles in the same segment of a circle. He has not got to spend time wondering which rule to apply, though he may have to think a little just how to apply it.

But when he comes to doing a Latin prose or a mixed selection of geometrical riders he has continually to be asking himself which is the appropriate rule to apply, which, to borrow a metaphor from golf, is the right club to use. We shall return later in this chapter to the question of the selection of the right rule.

So far our examples of the application of a rule have been chosen from the field of academic education, Latin and Mathematics. Similar principles apply to the use of practical rules of thought and action in an open system.

If a boy is being taught how to play cricket, for example, he is shown the strokes that are appropriate for different types of ball; the golfer is taught a basic swing and shown the different strokes and, literally, the different clubs that are appropriate to various situations; we are all taught when young the rules for tying ties, for keeping one's balance on a bicycle, for not getting hurt when we jump from a high wall and a whole host of others.

The test of these rules is on the whole that they work: we cannot say of most of them, as with the Latin sentence, that they might just as well have been different. If one made it a rule *not* to bend one's knees when jumping from a height the consequences would be painful, and if one made it a rule to play across and not down the line of the ball, bat would connect with ball less frequently. But as with the rules of Mathematics and language we do not want to have to think about them, far less to think them out, every time we use them. For most of us they become habits, rules of action which we apply without thought. Indeed in some cases, as notoriously in that of tying a tie, once we start consciously to think exactly what the rules are, we may find that we become muddled about it and are less able to perform the action properly. Our hands 'know' what the rule is but our minds have forgotten.

With the practical rules of an open system as with the rules of a closed one there may or may not be opportunities for initiative and scope for manoeuvre in the interpretation and application of the rules. An employee who is sitting at a factory bench applying the rule that the third knob from the right should be tightened up on a succession of articles that pass in front of him has no such scope. Whereas the personnel officer, who is applying rules that he has learnt for the promotion of harmonious relations inside the factory, has a great deal.

The ability to follow a narrow rule, perhaps a succession of narrow rules, blindly, not worrying whether they make sense or what their purpose is, may undoubtedly be useful on occasions. To teach people to do this is an essential part of education. There are many departments of life in which people are asked to do only this, as with the example just quoted at the factory bench, or at a rather more advanced level, when someone is looking figures up in tables and making appropriate simple calculations to work out navigational problems for an aeroplane. In the first example it would not be at all necessary to know what the knobs were for, though it might make the work more interesting; and in the

second example it would not be necessary to understand the
theory of the triangle of velocities on which the calculations
were based, and there is no reason why such understanding
should in any way increase the efficiency with which the process
was carried out.

Although it is not always possible, there is a tendency more
and more for the machine to take over in work, whether physical or mental, which can be reduced to the carrying out of a
simple rule. The processes of production are split up into simpler
and simpler operations and machines are designed to take them
over; and where the processes of thinking are capable of being
split up into stages which involve the application of simple rules
they too are being taken over by machines. Mechanical brains
are now being constructed which not merely carry out straightforward calculations, but which also have a memory and are
capable of rejecting a rule which is not applicable and selecting
one that is. The great advantage which machines have over
human beings is that they are almost always quicker, more
accurate and more reliable and usually in the long run cheaper.
But a machine can only do what it is taught to do, and it can
only be taught to do those things which a man in theory knows
how to do, although he is unlikely to be able to do them as quickly
as the machine. It is just because we can now make such efficient
thinking machines in our laboratories that it has become less and
less desirable to make them in our schools. Essential as it may be
to collect a large stock of rules in the course of one's education,
to know how to apply them and to know when to apply them,
this is not enough. What is needed is a greater flexibility of thinking and we shall return to this point later.

THE SELECTION AND ADAPTATION OF RULES

The man who tries to have a rule for every possible eventuality either of thought or action will inevitably have to collect a

very large number. The mathematician who wants a formula for every type of sum will have to put a considerable strain on his memory; he will probably not be generally considered a very good mathematician because it will always be possible to devise a question for which he has no formula, and if he has learnt to depend on them too closely he is likely to be at a loss. Golf is played nowadays with such carefully graded clubs that there is a different iron for differences in length of a mere 10 yards. But if a golfer is to equip himself with a club for every eventuality the burden will be too much for his caddy or his trolley. In fact the laws of golf now limit the number that may be carried to 14, but even so the game has become much more formalized than it was, in the sense that there is more and more of a tendency for the golfer just to vary the club and play the same stroke, instead of using the same club and varying the stroke. Like the mathematician who relies too much on formulae such a golfer may be at a loss when faced with an unusual situation.

The golfer with many clubs is not on the whole going to find it difficult to know which one to select: he has a rule for doing so. If he wants to hit the ball 160 yards he uses a No. 4 iron, if the distance is 170 yards he uses a No. 3. (There is a danger of course that if he judges the distance to be 165 yards he may have a nervous breakdown.)

The mathematician with a large number of formulae may find the selection rather harder because he will have more formulae than any golfer could possibly have clubs. But in principle what he is doing is the same. He has got to recognize what type of problem it is, he has got to remember what formulae he has available, and he has got to see which one is appropriate. With some types of mathematical problem, for example geometrical riders, seeing which is appropriate may be a very difficult thing to do.

The more specialized the rule or the club, the greater will be the number and the less the intelligence required. And conversely it is a commonplace that if one wants to teach an unintelligent person how to do mathematics, play chess or acquire some difficult skill, there will be a tendency to reduce the subject to a succession of simple rules or formulae. The stupid chess player will learn a great many traditional openings off by heart, whereas the more intelligent one will grasp the principles involved, will learn, as it were, wider, looser rules that he will be able to adapt to different circumstances and apply to whatever situations may arise with a greater chance of success: he will be a better chess player. Similarly the mathematician who remembers fewer formulae but has grasped more general principles is likely to be able to solve a greater variety of harder problems than the one who relies on a large accumulated store of formulae.

The stupid private soldier will be firmly disciplined or conditioned to react in a set way to set circumstances, but he will not be as good a soldier as the more intelligent man who can be fitted with a looser, wider set of rules with room for manoeuvre, so that he can adapt his action to different situations.

It is probably not in fact true that the golfer who uses only a few clubs but can play a greater variety of shots with each of them is likely to be more successful, in the sense of winning golf championships, than the man who has clubs for a greater variety of occasions, but we may well feel that he exhibits a greater degree of skill than his more mechanical rival.

If we turn to wider fields and consider for example the welfare worker dealing with human problems, it is obvious that it is impossible to have a specialized rule or formula for each set of circumstances that may arise. The system is an open one and no two sets of circumstances will be alike though there will be similarities. The worker has got to be able to apply and adapt general principles to particular situations: he may have some rough and ready formulae or rules but if he sticks to them and applies them too rigidly he will not be doing his job very well. We all know the mistakes that can be made by the Civil Servant who deals with human beings by rule of thumb and applies his rules and regulations too inflexibly and literally.

It is true in almost every department of thought and action that we are more likely to achieve long-term success if we use fewer, more general and fundamental principles and learn how to adapt them, than if we acquire a very large stock of specialized rules and formulae designed to apply to every possible eventuality.

CRITICISM OF A RULE

There are certain rules which are beyond criticism. The rule in Latin that the object should be put into the Accusative just is so, and we are not in a position to suggest an alternative and superior treatment of objects. Such a suggestion could only reasonably have been made when the Latin language was being formed. But there are many rules of thought and more especially of action which are and should be open to criticism. In any closed system, in mathematics or in chess, old methods and formulae may at any time be criticized, improved upon, and replaced. In open systems scientific hypotheses are found inadequate and replaced by new ones which stand up better to the tests of accuracy of prediction and explanation of the data; and in the practical affairs and problems of everyday life new methods and techniques are continually being devised, new rules evolved and applied. It is an essential part of progress that this should be so, and therefore that we should be prepared to analyse critically our old rules and methods.

In order to do this we must have a clear idea always of the object of the exercise, of what purpose the particular rule is designed to fulfil. We are more likely to have this, and to criticize effectively, if we have the ability to use general principles and adapt them to particular circumstances than if we are cluttered up with a large number of formulae. The person who thinks and acts in the framework of closely specialized rules is less likely to understand the basic principles and therefore more likely to regard his formulae as sacrosanct. He will not sufficiently often ask: 'What is this rule for? What are we trying to do? Is there a better method?'

The criticism of old rules clearly leads us on to the formation of new ones. Not unnaturally this is the hardest problem of all, and it will not be easy to suggest any rules for the discovery or construction of rules. Nevertheless this is a matter which it is essential to consider. Before we do so, however, it will be useful to illustrate various points by discussing the solution of a few specific problems.

A CAUSE-TRACING PROBLEM

Let us consider first an open-system problem. This is a question that was set as an example (6) in Chapter 8. The figures were given of the number of people who were convicted of smuggling goods through the Customs to avoid paying duty in various years, and the main facts were that in 1950–1 there were 2,293 convictions and in 1955–6 there were 1,123—a decrease of approximately 50%. What are the possible explanations of such a considerable change?

The effect here is given to us, we are searching for causes. The 'rules' we are going to apply will be fairly self-evident principles of human behaviour and we need of course to know something about how the Customs work and the sort of goods that people tend to try to smuggle through. These things are likely to be fairly general knowledge. The essential point about the investigation of this problem is that we must survey systematically and thoroughly all the causes that are theoretically possible: it might then be desirable to make some more enquiries to discover which of them are likely to operate in practice.

The number of convictions depends directly on the behaviour of two sets of people—travellers returning from abroad, and Customs officers. It must be possible to put the explanations under one or other (or possibly to some extent both) of two main headings:

(1) Fewer people have in fact been guilty of smuggling.
(2) The same number have been guilty, or possibly more, but fewer of them have been caught.

We can now investigate possible reasons for each of these main possibilities.

Suggestions for (1) are:

(a) That there have been fewer travellers.
(b) That people have become more honest.
(c) That the penalties have been increased and therefore people have been more frightened.
(d) That the rewards have been decreased; in other words people stand to save less by smuggling, and therefore people have been less tempted: this could be because the customs dues have been diminished in amount or in their range of application or because goods that previously used to be smuggled in (e.g. silk stockings, watches, cameras, food, wine) can now more easily and cheaply be procured in this country.

Possibilities under the second heading are:

(e) That people have become more skilful in avoiding detection.
(f) That there have been fewer Customs Officers and that searches have therefore been less thorough.
(g) That the Customs Officers have been less efficient and vigilant.
(h) That the Customs Officers have been corrupt and have been bribed to let things through.

Clearly we must not expect to find one simple cause: it is quite likely that several causes operate though there may be one over-riding one.

Having enumerated those which are theoretically possible the next step would be to decide whether any of them can be eliminated as matters of fact. Those which are susceptible to this kind of test are (*a*), (*c*), (*d*) and (*f*). It would not be hard to discover whether the number of travellers has increased or diminished, whether penalties have been increased, whether the suggested reasons for travellers being tempted less have operated, and what changes have taken place in the numbers of Customs Officers and the time they spend on an average in their searches.

One method that can sometimes be used in an enquiry of this kind is to take a sample of the people with whose actions and motives we are mainly concerned and ask them questions. But in this case the cross-examination of a sample of travellers as to whether they have become more honest, less skilful, more frightened or less tempted would not, for obvious reasons, be likely to provide very reliable information.

When more factual information had been obtained the en-quirer would be in a position to form an opinion as to which of the causes operated and to what extent. Our object here is to out-line a method of enquiry rather than produce a solution, but we would suggest that (*d*) is the factor to which most weight should probably be attached.

The important point about the tackling of this problem is the systematic examination of the factors (sets of people) involved, and the changes that can have taken place in their numbers, their actions and their motives for action. One has clearly got a better chance of solving the problem thoroughly if one sets out all the causes that are theoretically possible, and then eliminates those that can be seen not to operate, than if one merely looks for positive evidence as to what might have been the cause. This is not to say of course that in this particular problem, and others like it, there may not be many intelligent people who would arrive by using a positive method at as satisfactory a solution as would be reached more slowly by those who use the more laborious method. But to be more thorough is to be more certain, and the greater the complexity of the problem the more likely it is that the systematic, methodical approach will get nearer to the truth.

A THEORETICAL PROBLEM

We will consider now a problem of a very different kind.
'Smith lives in 13th Avenue which has houses numbered from 13 to 1,300. Jones wants to know the number of Smith's house.

'Jones asks: "Is it less than 500?"
            'Smith answers, but he lies.
'Jones asks: "Is it a perfect square?"
            'Smith answers, but he lies.
'Jones asks: "Is it a perfect cube?"
            'Smith answers and he tells the truth.
'Jones says: "If I knew whether the second figure was 1, I could tell you the number of the house."
'Smith tells him and Jones announces the number of the house, but he is wrong.
'What was the number of Smith's house?'

This is a problem which is completely in a closed system. Obviously we must know about numbers and squares and cubes, but there can be no question here of searching for fresh data or of testing the solution against any outside factors. Also if there is a solution it must be unique, and from the fact that the question or puzzle has been set at all we shall certainly expect there to be a definitely discoverable answer.

Let us see how to set about finding it.

From the questions asked by Jones and from Smith's answers it is clearly not possible to come to any conclusion at all as to whether the number is or is not less than 500, a perfect square or a perfect cube: to start with, considered by themselves, they tell us precisely nothing. The only thing that can possibly give us a starting point is the statement by Jones: 'If I knew whether the second figure was 1, I could tell you the number of the house.'

At first sight this may not seem to be very informative: we are not told what Smith tells him about this and even if we were it would not help much as in any case the number that Jones announces is wrong.

If we look at the statement however from the point of view of what it tells us about Jones's state of mind we see that the information it gives us might be very helpful. Jones is in a position where he thinks he has reduced the possible alternatives to two and one of them has 1 as its second figure. We know in fact that Jones is wrong but nevertheless this is a line worth pursuing.

Jones must think, however erroneously, that he knows whether the number is less than 500, a perfect square, or a perfect cube. If he were to think that it was neither a square nor a cube he could clearly not have reduced the alternatives to two. Again if he were to think that it was a square and not a cube there would be far too many alternatives (the squares of all numbers from 4 to 22 inclusive lie between 13 and 500, and of all numbers from 23 to 36 inclusive between 500 and 1300). It looks therefore as though he must think that the number is a cube.

It is easy to calculate that the relevant cubes are: 27, 64, 125, 216, 343, 512, 729, 1,000. (They are the cubes of 3, 4, 5, 6, 7, 8, 9, 10.) Of these 64 and 729 are also squares (of 8 and 27 respectively). Clearly the numbers that are cubes of perfect squares (i.e. of 4 and 9) will also be perfect squares themselves.

We see now that if Jones were to think that the number was a perfect square *and* a perfect cube less than 500 there would be no alternative, it would have to be 64. Similarly, if he were to think it a perfect square *and* a perfect cube greater than 500, it would have to be 729. If he were to think it a perfect cube and not a perfect square less than 500 there would be four possibilities (27, 125, 216, 343); but if he were to think it a perfect cube and not a perfect square above 500 there are only two possibilities, 512 and 1,000 one of which has 1 as its second figure.

This, then, is what Jones must think.

But he thinks in certain respects incorrectly. He thinks it is not less than 500, but Smith lied to him about this, so in reality it is less than 500. He thinks it is not a perfect square, but Smith lied to him about this too, so that it really is a perfect square. He thinks it is a perfect cube and as Smith told him the truth about this a perfect cube it is.

The correct number of Smith's house is therefore a perfect square and a perfect cube less than 500. There is only one such number which is greater than 13 and that is 64, which is therefore the solution.

It has been thought worth while to explain the method and the reasoning required for the solution of this problem in some detail. It is clearly a highly artificial one, but nevertheless is not completely irrelevant to real life. The important and interesting thing is to see that a conclusion is possible on apparently slender evidence, and how it is necessary to feel round for a starting point. The detective or the criminologist knows how important it is to squeeze the last drop out of the evidence, and there are a great many departments of ordinary life where it may be useful to infer someone's state of mind and the sources of his information from what he said. In an open-system problem, however, one is unlikely to know whether there is a solution and if so how definite it can be, and one must be very careful to resist the temptation to infer too much, to squeeze from the evidence more than is really there, in fact to act as though one were a detective in a story and be a bit too clever.

A 'COURSE-OF-ACTION' PROBLEM

Let us consider now a problem of a different type where the question is to decide on a course of action.

Suppose a situation where the owner of a small private business is wondering whether to instal more up-to-date machinery. Some of his rivals have done so and have shown signs that they will as a result be enabled to undercut him. His labour costs have risen steeply and with this machinery he will be able to produce the same volume of goods with the employment of several fewer people. Allowing for the interest to be paid on the capital used to buy the machines, their running cost, and the amount to be set aside for depreciation, he reckons that without any doubt there will be a considerable net saving.

On the other hand his employees are very conservative and he knows that they will not react favourably to the introduction of new-fangled methods. Also they have all been in his employment for a long time and he would be very reluctant to dismiss any of them, not only because of the distress caused to those who go but also because of the distressing and unsettling effect on those who are left. Others might give notice; he might find it difficult to get the same quality of staff; the atmosphere which he has built up of loyalty and co-operative hard work might be disturbed. What is he to do?

Clearly it is not possible to suggest a solution without more detailed information about the facts, figures, and personalities involved. But two important points emerge.

In the first place this is quite clearly a problem to which there is no cut-and-dried, uniquely right solution. A value judgement has got to be made in which the short- and long-term financial advantages of the new machinery have got to be set against the disadvantages on the personal side. An ingenious and tactful managing director may be able to minimize these disadvantages, perhaps he can persuade his staff how much easier the machinery will make their lives, perhaps he can think out ways of maintaining the atmosphere which he seems to be in danger of losing. But in the last resort a decision has got to be made in which unlike things are balanced against each other: he will be able to see how his chosen solution works out, but he will never be able to tell that it was the 'best' one, though he can certainly form an opinion about it, for he will never know what would have been the outcome of other solutions.

Secondly it is worth noting a tendency in a problem of this type for people to say that 'logically' the right thing to do would be to install the machinery but that this solution would neglect the human factor, and therefore, by implication, what a lot of shortcomings 'logic' has. To say this would be, of course, to use the word logic in a very odd sense. To neglect the human factor would be to leave out a vital part of the data of the problem, and to produce a solution to a problem without considering all the data is not a logical but a highly illogical thing to do.

'APPRECIATING THE SITUATION'

A main point that emerged from the consideration of the problem about smuggling was the desirability, if the problem is at all complex, of having a systematic method of approach. We are taught when writing out a geometrical theorem to set out clearly what it is that we know about the figure and what it is that we are trying to prove. Similarly anyone who has had any military training will know that the method which the officer or N.C.O. is encouraged to use when faced with a tactical problem is that of thinking out, and if possible setting down, a systematic 'Appreciation of the situation'. The particular details of the military way of doing this are designed to apply to a state of affairs when there is a conflict between two parties (as in a game of chess) and will largely comprise a summary of the courses open

o

to both sides. But there are many problems in both closed and open systems where it will be profitable to set down exactly what the situation is as far as it is known, exactly what it is that we are trying to do or to discover, and a list of the theoretically possible solutions—causes of the effect, perhaps, if we are trying to find why something happened, or effects of a cause or a complex of causes if we are trying to forecast something that is going to happen.

To do this of course is not to solve the problem, but it is a useful preliminary which may make a solution easier to find. It will often lead to a solution by elimination, for with a list of the possibilities in front of us we may be able to strike out for various reasons all but one or two and thus reach at least a tentative answer which we could not have achieved by a more positive, direct approach.

The precise method and form which it will be desirable to use for making our attack on the problem a systematic one will vary greatly. To try to lay down rules for different types of questions would be like trying to provide the mathematician with formulae for all the different types of sums he may be asked to do. But the general principle is clear and important. Just as we might advise the housewife to be tidy for easier living without telling her exactly where to put everything, so we advise the thinker to be systematic for easier problem-solving without telling him what system to use on each occasion.

CONSTRUCTING A RULE

To apply rules, to select and adapt rules, to criticize rules: these three things are in ascending order of difficulty, and require an ascending order of intelligence. But the hardest thing, which requires the most intelligence as well as being the most important, is to construct rules where none were before; to devise a method for attacking the new, the unfamiliar problem.

It is hardly to be expected that it would be possible to supply rules for doing this, but there are certain observations that may usefully be made about it. In order to solve the stubborn, unfamiliar problem, in order to construct a rule for dealing with that for which no rule exists, it is necessary above all things to be on one's intellectual toes, to be prepared to look for new ways of untying the knot instead of picking away at the same bit of string. Or, to use another analogy, if one wants to get to the heart of an apparently impenetrable thicket where no one has been before one must be prepared to walk round it, search for new approaches and not keep hacking away at the same point. Sometimes, to pursue the analogy further, it may be sensible to start along a path that appears temporarily to be leading away from the objective in the hope or expectation that it will twist in the right direction. On the other hand it may be important to resist the temptation to take any path wherever it is going in preference to continually fighting one's way through the undergrowth.

The essential points are to rely on general principles rather than specialized rules, to be able to stand back from the problem and be flexible in one's thinking, to beware of preconceived notions, and to be very conscious the whole time of exactly what it is that one is trying to do. Some people have a capacity for 'seeing' the solution, whether it is of a chess problem, a mathematical problem, or a complex practical problem, just as some people have an 'instinct' for finding their way about in the jungle. But this ability to see, or this instinct, are usually derived from experience and practice in just this art of probing the unknown. It is certainly not true to say that either one can or one can't, it is an ability that can to a considerable extent be acquired.

Here are two examples of problems in which 'the other way round', new ways of looking at things, may be helpful. The first one is very simple and trivial, the second very complicated and important.

Suppose a man is asked to find a number between 500 and 1,000 which goes exactly into 5,000. From the way the question is put the first obvious thing to do is to look, as it were, at the numbers between 500 and 1,000. There are rather a lot of them, however, and it will be more fruitful to reflect that if there is a number between 500 and 1,000 which goes exactly into 5,000 it must go between 10 and 5 times. The numbers there are between 10 and 5 are 9, 8, 7 and 6: the only one of these which is a factor of 5,000 is 8, and 8 goes into 5,000, 625 times. 625 is therefore the answer.

The lesson of this is not to allow one's method of solution to be dictated by the form in which the question has been put.

Consider now a more practical and very topical example. At the time of writing (April 1957) a Royal Commission is about to investigate our monetary and financial system. What they are being asked to do is to consider how satisfactorily the system is working at present, and to make recommendations for its improvement.

What must be the method of these Commissioners and what do they need in order to be successful?

They must first have a very clear idea of what it is they are trying to do. Ends and means must be clearly separated in their minds. What is it that the monetary system is for? Do the separate parts of which it is composed, and all the complicated processes which go on there, contribute towards promoting these ends? Or are they just there because they have been there for a long time, their use and their function have not been questioned, and they are now regarded as ends in themselves rather than as means to a more important end?

They must clearly have a detailed knowledge of how the system works. This will not be easy, because the system is vastly complicated and the interconnection of causes and effects may be exceedingly difficult to trace. In their investigation of exactly how the system works it will be important for them not to be burdened too much with preconceived ideas, but to be capable of looking at things freshly and to derive a great deal of information from the examination of witnesses. But in examining them it will be essential to remember that their views are likely to be partial, that they are probably not in a position to explain how any part of the machine excepting their own works, or to evaluate the precise significance of their part of the machine in the working of the whole. They have to consider to what extent the old rules satisfactorily performed their supposed functions and to what extent newly devised rules might perform them better. What they have to do in fact is an exceedingly difficult intellectual exercise, and it would be optimistic to hope that they will arrive at the best solution.

What processes of education are most likely to produce people capable of solving such an immensely complicated theoretical and practical problem? We have seen that stocks of rules are essential, but it is suggested that it is even more essential to give practice in solving unusual intellectual problems, both theoretical and practical; practice in other words in devising new rules for unfamiliar situations.

One of the dilemmas about education is that however difficult a subject may at first sight appear to be, however much it may appear to provide mental exercise and opportunities for those who study it to use their minds, rather than their memories and the stereotyped application of simple rules, each subject in turn and each new branch of it eventually become formalized. Those who make it formalized are using their minds in the best possible way. They are solving the new problems, devising the new rules, and in so far as the solution of these problems leads to practical advantages they are rendering valuable services to the community. But unfortunately they are at the same time removing from the subject much of its advantage as an educational instrument. The more formalized it becomes, the more the processes of thinking are broken down into intermediate parts and the more closely the links in the chain of reasoning are examined, the easier it will be to think along those lines and arrive at the right conclusions. But the harder it will be for those who have been trained merely in a subject which has already become formalized to turn their minds to the devising of new rules for problems which have hitherto been unsolved. It is interesting that Intelligence Tests, which were designed partly to discover the ability of those tested to solve the unfamiliar problem, to devise a new rule because none of those they had were applicable, are in danger of becoming formalized.

This is an exceedingly difficult educational dilemma to which there is no simple solution. Perhaps the most important thing is to realize its existence, and to appreciate the fact that, necessary as it undoubtedly is to acquire much knowledge and a vast store of theoretical and practical rules, something more is required for a complete education.

Examples on Chapter 10

1. $p \; \mathsf{Y} \; q$ means that if p is red, q is red,
   if p is pink, q is blue,
   if p is blue, q is pink.

   $p \; \nearrow \; q$ means that if p is red, q is pink,
   if p is pink, q is blue,
   if p is blue, q is red.

   $p \; \swarrow \; q$ means that if p is red, q is blue,
   if p is pink, q is pink,
   if p is blue, q is red.

You are told that:

$$p \, \curlyvee \, q \, \nearrow \, r \, \curlyvee \, s \, \swarrow \, t \, \nearrow \, x \, \curlyvee \, y \, \nearrow \, z \, \swarrow \, l \, \curlyvee \, m$$

If *p* is pink, what colour is *m*?

2. The total number of people who watched the County Cricket Championship in 1949 was 2,126,000, and in 1956 the figure was 1,174,000.

Make an analysis of the possible reasons for this decline, and consider what further investigations you would need to make in order to come to some conclusion about the most likely causes.

3. Mr. and Mrs. Smith, Mr. and Mrs. Brown and Mr. and Mrs. Green, are seated equally spaced round a circular table. No man is sitting next to his wife, but each lady has a man on each side of her.

The names of the men and their wives, not necessarily respectively, are Tom, Dick and Harry, and Nancy, Joan and Mary. The occupations of the men, again not necessarily respectively, are architect, politician and dustman.

Dick and Mr. Smith often play bridge with the architect's wife and Mrs. Green.

The dustman, who is an only child, has Mary on his right.

The politician is sitting nearer to Nancy than he is to Mrs. Brown.

Harry is the architect's brother-in-law, and he has his only sister sitting on his left. The architect is sisterless.

Find their names, their occupations, and the order in which they are sitting round the table.

4. There are three men, Smith, Jones and Brown.

Smith says: 'Brown is heavier than I am, and Brown is also heavier than Jones.'

Jones says: 'I am heavier than Smith, and Smith is heavier than Brown.'

Brown says: 'Smith is heavier than I am, and Jones weighs the same as I do.'

Assuming that the lighter a person is the more likely he is to tell the truth, arrange Smith, Jones and Brown, in order of heaviness.

5. The estimated population of the United Kingdom in June 1957 was 51,657 thousand. The distribution among the various age-groups was as follows (figures represent thousands):

0—4	3,907	30—34	3,591	60—64	2,573
5—9	4,031	35—39	3,630	65—69	2,147
10—14	4,022	40—44	3,602	70—74	1,692
15—19	3,303	45—49	3,739	75—79	1,170
20—24	3,281	50—54	3,543	80—84	627
25—29	3,403	55—59	3,097	85 and over	299

(i) How do these figures differ from what you would expect if the same number of people were born each year? Try to account for these differences.

(ii) What do you think is the effect of Immigration and Emigration on these figures?

(iii) Make an appreciation of the situation from the point of view of the Ministry of Education.

6. In 1921 approximately 1,300,000 out of the United Kingdom population of 58,000,000 were over 70 (about 3·4%). Use the data of question 5 to find the corresponding figures for 1957.

Discuss the reasons for and the consequences of the trend shown by these figures. Do you think the trend will be continued in the future?

7. There are five men, A, B, C, D, E, each of whom has a white or a black disc attached to his forehead. Each man can see the discs worn by the other four, but is unable to see his own. If a man is wearing a white disc, any statement he makes is true; if he is wearing a black disc, any statement he makes is false. Statements are made as follows:

A says: 'I see three white discs and one black.'

B says: 'I see four black discs.'

C says: 'I see one white disc and three black discs.'

E says: 'I see four white discs.'

Deduce the colours of the discs worn by all five men.

8. John, James, Nancy, Lucy and Pamela made statements as follows:

John: Nancy is my wife; James is my son; Pamela is my aunt.

James: Lucy is my sister; Pamela is my mother; Pamela is John's sister.

Nancy: I have no brothers or sisters; John is my son; John has a son.

Lucy: I have no children; Nancy is my sister; John is my brother.

Pamela: John is my nephew; Lucy is my niece; Nancy is my daughter.

Assuming that

(1) anyone who has one or more brothers or sisters *and* one or more children *always* tells the truth;

(2) anyone who has *either* one or more brothers or sisters *or* one or more children makes statements which are alternately true and false;

(3) anyone who has no brothers or sisters and no children never tells the truth;

find which of the above statements are true and what relations these five people are to each other.

9. Discuss the problems of road safety and congestion on the roads of this country with reference to the following approximate figures:

	1938	1955
Number of Motor Vehicles	3,000,000	6,000,000
Mileage of Public Roads	180,000	188,000
Number of persons killed in road accidents	6,600	5,500

10. In a certain community the membership of the Buffer Club is composed of all those over 70 who are not toothless, of all toothless people who are not members of the Nashum Club and of all members of the Nashum Club who are not over 70.

Can you tell whether a man is a member of the Nashum Club if you are told he is:

(i) over 70, toothless, not a member of the Buffer Club?

(ii) under 70, possessed of teeth, not a member of the Buffer Club?

(iii) under 70, toothless, a member of the Buffer Club?

11. In the Utopia Factory there are 7 employees—Alf, Bert,

Charlie, Duggie, Ernie, Fred, and George. The Factory has full work-ing days on Monday, Tuesday, Thursday and Friday and a half work-ing day on Wednesday. The Factory's rules are as follows:

(i) The Bottle-Washer must always be present.

(ii) At least 2 employees must be absent each day.

(iii) Bert must never be absent on the day after Alf is present unless Duggie is absent too, in which case both Bert and George must be absent.

Those present more than $2\frac{1}{2}$ days always tell the truth.

Those present less than $2\frac{1}{2}$ days never tell the truth.

Those present exactly $2\frac{1}{2}$ days make statements which are alter-nately true and false.

(Wednesday is the only day on which employees may work half a day.)

They make statements as follows:

Alf   (1) Duggie and Ernie are equally truthful.

        (2) George is the Bottle-Washer.

Bert   (1) I wasn't there on Wednesday.

        (2) George is never absent when Ernie is.

Charlie (1) Bert and Duggie are equally truthful.

        (2) Bert was there on Wednesday.

Duggie (1) Fred was only absent on Wednesday.

        (2) I was there for less than $2\frac{1}{2}$ days.

Ernie   (1) Alf and I are never present together or absent to-gether.

        (2) I wasn't there on Tuesday or Wednesday.

Fred   (1) Ernie always tells the truth.

        (2) Duggie was there on Monday and Tuesday.

George (1) I wasn't there on Wednesday.

        (2) Duggie always tells the truth.

Who was present when? Who is the Bottle-Washer?

12. The Utopia Factory still has the same 7 employees: their names are Alf, Bert, Charlie, Duggie, Ernie, Fred and George. Their jobs, not necessarily respectively, are: Door-Opener, Door-Shutter, Door-Knob Polisher, Bottle-Washer, Sweeper-Upper, Welfare Officer, and Worker. The Door-Knob Polisher and the Sweeper-Upper never tell the truth; the Door-Opener and the Door-Shutter make statements

which are alternately true and false: the other three always tell the truth.

Their wages per week are now and have always been an exact number of shillings: no one gets more than £20 per week.

They make statements as follows:

Alf   (1) I get 20% more than Bert.

          (2) Bert gets 5% more than Ernie.

Bert   (1) Fred is the Welfare Officer.

          (2) I am not the Door-Opener.

Charlie (1) George is the Bottle-Washer.

          (2) The Door-Knob Polisher gets 15s. more than the Worker who gets 20% more than the Sweeper-Upper.

Duggie (1) I get 10s. more than the Welfare Officer who gets $33\frac{1}{3}$% more than he used to.

          (2) Alf gets more than George.

Ernie (1) Alf had an 8% rise this week.

          (2) The Door-Opener gets 20% less than the Worker.

Fred   (1) Charlie is the Worker.

          (2) The Door-Shutter is the best paid of us all.

George (1) I am not the Worker.

          (2) Bert is the Sweeper-Upper.

          (3) Ernie gets 5s. less than the Door-Knob Polisher who gets 10s. less than Fred.

Find the wages and occupation of each man.

13. The employees of the previous example have just woken from a long winter's slumber.

Their names are still Alf, Bert, Charlie, Duggie, Ernie, Fred and George, but they not only don't know where they are, they also don't know who they are, what their occupations are or who their wives are.

But the subconscious works wonders. Certain remarks are made, all in the third person, and any remark which anyone makes in which his own name comes is false, while anything he says about anybody else is true.

Their occupations are, but not necessarily respectively, Door-Knob Polisher, Door-Opener, Door-Shutter, Bottle-Washer, Sweeper-Upper, Welfare Officer, and Worker. And their wives' names are Agnes, Beatrice, Clarissa, Diana, Ethel, Flossie and Gertie. No man has the same first letter to his name as his wife has. Below are 21 numbered remarks. Each man makes three, and the total of the numbers of each man's remarks is the same, except for Duggie and Fred who are each one out.

(1) Ernie is the Worker. (2) Fred is not the Door-Opener. (3) Gertie is married to the Welfare Officer. (4) Clarissa's husband is the Door-Knob Polisher. (5) Bert is not the Door-Opener. (6) George is married to Diana. (7) Agnes is not married to Bert. (8) Duggie is the Worker. (9) Charlie's wife is Flossie. (10) Clarissa is married to Bert. (11) Duggie is married to Beatrice. (12) Alf is the Bottle-Washer. (13) Charlie is the Door-Opener. (14) George is the Door-Knob Polisher. (15) George is not the Door-Shutter. (16) Charlie is the Door-Shutter. (17) Ernie is the Welfare Officer. (18) Ernie is married to Gertie. (19) The numbers of two of Bert's remarks are perfect squares. (20) Charlie is the Bottle-Washer. (21) Fred is the Door-Opener.

Find out for each man his occupation (which is not necessarily the same as in question 12), the name of his wife, and which remarks he makes.

14. A, B, and C, live in different houses in Abracadabra Avenue, which has houses numbered from 1–80. Their numbers ascend in the order A, B, C, but they none of them know this; nor do any of them know the numbers of the houses of the other two.

They are having a conversation about it.

A thinks that B always tells the truth, and that C always lies.

B thinks that C always tells the truth, and that A always lies.

C thinks that A always tells the truth and that B always lies.

Each one announces, not necessarily correctly, whether his number is (i) a multiple of 4, (ii) a perfect square, (iii) above 23.

A then says to B and C: 'I can tell you the numbers of your two houses, but I don't know which is which.'

B says to A: 'I can tell you the number of your house.'

C says to B: 'I can tell you the number of your house.'

They all do so, but they are all wrong: and in fact of the numbers announced, not one is the number of any of the three houses, though one of them is exactly eight times the number of one of the houses. Where do A, B and C live?

Solutions

1. To say this is to get things the wrong way round. The animals (pigs) are not so called because they are dirty, but the word 'pig' bears a connotation of uncleanness because the animals (pigs) are reputed to have dirty habits. Animals (other than pigs) or human beings may then be called pigs as a term of abuse because they are dirty.

2. (i) A more likely conclusion would be that the boys are referring to different things. (In fact they are, as a subsequent passage from the book quoted shows.)

(ii) Not for exactly the same article. It may be useful to have different words for articles which differ slightly.

3. An example of exaggerated and superstitious importance being attached to words.

5. (i) Unlikely to be effective. Many other things have yellow skins.

(ii) Some chance of being effective: the skin of a banana has some, but not many, other properties besides that of being yellow (e.g. of being thick, easy to remove).

(iii) Likely to be effective. A banana has nothing other than its skin which is yellow.

6. Obviously one must use the objects one has for ostensive definition and try to find ideas in the native's mind which are closely akin to those for which the words stand. If the natives do not use money the task of explaining the meaning of the word is probably hopeless.

7. The connotation, if there is any doubt, can be discovered from a dictionary. Notice that the denotation of 'centaur' is nil, the class of centaurs is an empty one. The denotation of 'John Smith' is all those people who bear that name, the connotation is simply the characteristic of having that name.

8. (i) The kind of power to which knowledge leads is on the whole

man's mastery over nature, derived from scientific knowledge. The kind of power which is usually thought of as corrupting is political power, power over people. Such power is not usually derived from knowledge, though it may be.

(ii) 'To promote the interests' of somebody usually means 'to do something to their advantage'. 'Interests' in the second sentence clearly means activities, hobbies, things in which an interest is taken. It may or may not be to the interest (advantage) of those I love to have their interests (activities) encouraged.

(iii) In '... bestowed ... liberally', 'liberally endowed', 'liberally' means generously, lavishly. A 'liberal' education means one which is wide, not narrowly scientific. A 'liberal' point of view (not, notice, Liberal, which would of course be that of the Liberal Party) is one which is not narrow or rigid, but progressive and taking into account a variety of opinions.

Although these meanings have something in common they differ sufficiently to stultify the argument completely.

(iv) In the first sentence 'right' means 'morally right': in 'rightly applied' it means 'correctly'. In deciding whether the application is right (correct) there is no reason why we should apply the same test as we used for rightness (moral rightness) of the original action.

(v) The referee's 'view ... is ... partial' means that he cannot see everything. That the referee should be 'impartial' in his decisions means that he should not be swayed by irrelevant considerations such as that a friend of his is playing for one side. There is not much connection between these meanings.

9. 'Cow' would certainly not be plainer unless it had been made so by ostensive definition. And this is the point that Dr. Johnson seems to be making—that ostensive definition ('I *see* a cow') is to be preferred to verbal definition, and that verbal definition may be an obstruction to understanding and not an aid.

For the ordinary person who is interested merely in recognizing cows this may be true; for the biologist or scientist who wants to know more about cows—their characteristics, their connotation—it is certainly not true.

CHAPTER 3

1. (i) 'Not all' would be more likely to mean 'nearly all'.

(ii) The meaning is the same.

(iii) The original says two things: that those under 14 are allowed to travel at half-fare, and that no one else is. The revised version does not specifically state the first of these. Another sentence would have to be added: 'Persons under 14 are persons who are allowed to travel at half-fare'.

(iv) The original might be used to encourage someone who is not an expert, an implication which it would be harder for the revised version to carry.

(v) 'Few' gives more precise information than 'some'. It might be amended to: 'The proportion of Englishmen-who-have-been-to-Russia is a small proportion.' A very artificial way of saying a simple thing.

2. Use Euler's circles. It will be seen that the conclusion does not follow. It is not possible to deduce whether there are any Socialists in favour of Free Trade or Liberals in favour of Capital Punishment.

3. Use Euler's circles. Those who voted for D may or may not have voted for E; none of them voted for either A or B.

4. All Bald men are Aristocrats, Draughts Players and Ethiopians; but not all Aristocrats, Draughts Players or Ethiopians are Bald. Some Aristocrats are neither Draughts Players nor Ethiopians, and some Draughts Players are neither Aristocrats nor Ethiopians. No Chess Players are either Bald or Ethiopian. All Chess Players are Aristocrats. Some Chess Players, but not all, are Draughts Players.

5. All of these are used more often as contraries than as contradictories.

6.   (i) *Contradictory*   Some Communists are not knaves.
        Contrary   No Communists are knaves.
  (ii) *Contradictory*   No express trains arrive on time.
        Contrary   Only goods trains arrive on time (assuming that no goods trains are express trains).
  (iii) *Contradictory*   A stitch in time does not save nine.
        Contrary   A stitch in time saves eight.

(iv) *Contradictory* Some pigs can fly.
     Contrary   All pigs can fly.

(v) *Contradictory*   All people are honest about their Income Tax.

     Contrary   The only thing that people are dishonest about is their Car Licences.

(vi) (The original means something like: 'Lanes with no turnings are apt to appear long.')

     Contradictory   Lanes with no turnings are not apt to appear long.

     Contrary   Lanes with no turnings are apt to appear of medium length.

(vii) *Contradictory* Not only Irishmen eat snails.
     Contrary   Only Welshmen eat snails.

(viii) (The original means that a sauce which is served with a goose is suitable also for serving with a gander. It is normally used to imply that treatment which is appropriate for A is also appropriate for B, and is often employed with a triumphant note when the treatment is some punishment or penalty which is now being administered to its erstwhile administrator).

     Contradictory   What's sauce for the goose is not sauce for the gander, (or what is appropriate for A is not also appropriate for B).

     Contrary   What's sauce for the goose is sauce also for only one other brand of meat and that's turkey, (or what is appropriate for A is appropriate also only for C).

(ix) (The original would normally be used poetically or emotively to express the importance of beautiful things and their appreciation. It might be paraphrased as: 'All works of Beauty express some aspect of the fundamental truth of things.')

     Contradictory   Beauty is not Truth.
     Contrary   Beauty is sometimes Truth.
                 (or 'Some works of Beauty express . . . etc.)

(Whether this or any other proposition is accepted as a

contrary depends on the way in which the very vague terms involved are being used in the particular context. This can only be discovered by a cross-examination of the writer or speaker.)

(x) *Contradictory*   I've not lost my hat.

       Contrary   I've got my hat in my hand.

7. (i)   (ii)   (iii)   (iv)

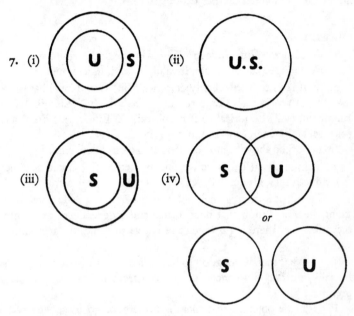

8. (i) Equivalent; (ii) Contradictory; (iii) Contradictory; (iv) Contrary; (v) Contrary.

9. (*a*) (v) is equivalent to (i).

       (iv) and (vii) can be inferred from (i).

   (*b*) (vi) and (xi) are contradictory to (v).

       (viii), (x) and (xii) are contradictory to (vii).

   (*c*) (ii) has no contrary.

       (v) and (ix) ar contrary to (iii),

       (i) and (v) are contrary to (xii).

10. Use Euler's circles. All, some or none of those who are in favour of lowering the school-leaving age could be Quakers. It is true that some professional musicians, at least those who are Welshmen, are not in favour of lowering the school-leaving age.

11. The Oddities Club is composed of all members of the Eccentrics Club who are not bald-headed and all bald-headed men who are not members of the Eccentrics Club.

CHAPTER 4

1. *Conclusions:* True, Indeterminate, Untrue, Indeterminate.
   Reasoning: Indeterminate, Invalid, Invalid, Indeterminate.

2. (i) Analytic, (ii) Probably empirical, (iii) Could be either: more likely to be analytic, (iv) Empirical, (v) Analytic, (vi) (Emotive), (vii) Empirical, (viii) Empirical, (ix) Empirical, (x) Either, (xi) Empirical, (xii) (Metaphorical), (xiii) Empirical, (xiv) Analytic.

(Many of the above could be different in certain contexts.)

3. (i) Inductive, (ii) Deductive, (iii) Inductive, (iv) Could be either, (v) Inductive, (vi) Inductive, (vii) Deductive.

4. The Proposition is analytic. The reasoning is deductive. If we grant the assumption that dependence and independence are contradictories, that there is no other alternative possible, the reasoning is valid.

5. (i) That there is no good to be spoken of the Irish. (It might also be said that this is a conclusion derived from the two statements as premisses.)

It might be objected that there *is* some good to be spoken of the Irish, namely that they are a 'Fair People'. The argument therefore is not entirely valid.

(ii) That he does not 'glitter' (i.e. is not very prepossessing, charming, has not much to say for himself). The 'argument' would be more convincing if he were able to point out that all that does not glitter is gold, which is a very different thing.

(iii) That it is sensible to vote for the Tories. Granted the premisses the argument is valid, but 'sensible' is being used to mean 'those who agree with me'.

CHAPTER 5

1. The equivalent groups are:
   (*a*) (i), (ii), (viii), (xv); (*b*) (iii), (ix), (xi), (xiv); (*c*) (iv), (vii), (xii), (xvi); (*d*) (v), (vi), (x), (xiii).

2. Valid.

3. (i) True; (ii) False; (iii) True, false.

4. *r* is false, *x* is true, *p* and *s* undetermined.

5. *p* and *r* are false, *q* is true, *s* undetermined.

6. (i) Smith has never played Croquet in Czechoslovakia, and is not a member of the Eccentric Sportsmen's Club; he is a member of the Oddfellows Association.

(ii) Jones is a founder member of the Hoop Club, a member of the Eccentrics Club, and has played Polo in Patagonia; he is not a member of the Oddfellows Association.

(iii) Robinson has not played Croquet in Czechoslovakia, is not a founder member of the Hoop Club or a member of the Eccentric Sportsmen's Club. He is a member of the Oddfellows Association.

7. *p, q, r* and *x* are true, *s* is false.

11. In the front porch.

12. (ii), (iv), (vi) are equivalent to each other.
    (iii), (v), (vii), (viii) are equivalent to each other.

13. (i) Untrue, (ii) True, (iii) True.

14. (i) A grifficorn. False; (ii) A pomox. True.

15. (i) Valid.

(ii) Argument invalid. There is the implication that 'people who smoke' are 'those who are unable to give up smoking', whereas they may just not want to; there is also the implication, which is certainly false, that 'brave people' and 'those who have weak characters' are clear-cut classes. If these implications were true, however, the argument would be formally valid.

(iii) Argument invalid. The first two sentences state that it is sensible to philosophize, the next sentence states that it is sensible to live a simple life. Even if 'simplicity' as applied to philosophy meant the same thing as 'living a simple life', which it clearly doesn't, it would not at all follow that simplicity was the essence of good philosophy.

16. The argument assumes that 'just' and 'unjust', 'loving' and 'hating' are pairs of contradictories. If this assumption and the premisses are granted the argument is perfectly sound and there is no disagreement between the two conclusions: either the gods hate him and men love him, or men hate him and the gods love him.

17. (i) Tautologous, (ii) Contingent, (iii) Tautologous, (iv) Self-contradictory, (v) Tautologous, (vi) Contingent, (vii) Self-contradictory, (viii) Tautologous, (ix) Contingent.

18. (i) Every day, (ii) Every day except Sunday, (iii) Saturday, (iv) Monday, Tuesday, (v) No day, (vi) Every day except Sunday.

19.   (i) After 5 p.m.
     (ii) Between 7 a.m. and 8 a.m.; between 9 a.m. and 10 a.m.
     (iii) Between noon and 5 p.m.; after 6 p.m.

20.   (i) John Jones, on May 10th; Sidney Smith, on March 4th.
     (ii) Caesar, between 7 p.m. and 8 p.m.

21. Between 40 and 45.

22. I may or may not have had bacon for breakfast. I certainly did not have kippers or sausages.

23. $\sim(p \supset \sim q)$.   24. $\sim(\sim p \lor \sim q)$.

25. $(\sim p \cdot q)$.

CHAPTER 6

1. (i) Yes. $S\,e\,P$. (ii) Yes. $S\,i\,P$. (iii) No. (iv) Yes. $S\,o\,P$. (v) No. (vi) Yes. $S\,e\,P$.

2. (i) No. Undistributed middle.

$$\frac{M\,i\,P}{S\,i\,M}$$
$$\overline{S\,i\,P}$$

(ii) No. Remember that 'some' does not exclude 'all'. A valid conclusion would be 'Some Europeans do not eat garlic'.

$$\frac{M\,o\,P}{M\,a\,S}$$
$$\overline{S\,i\,P}$$

(iii) Yes.

$$\frac{P\,e\,M}{M\,i\,S}$$
$$\overline{S\,o\,P}$$

(iv) No. Undistributed middle.

$$P \; a \; M$$
$$M \; i \; S$$
$$\overline{S \; i \; P}$$

3. (i) 'All actions which cause Inflation are against the long-term interests of the workers (unstated);
all increases in wages are actions which cause Inflation;
therefore all increases in wages are against the long-term interests of the workers.'
Formally valid.

(ii) 'All illegal actions are actions which are likely to lead to prosecution; (unstated),
travelling 1st class with a 2nd class ticket is an illegal action; (unstated),
therefore travelling 1st class with a 2nd class ticket is likely to lead to prosecution.'
Valid.

(iii) For the syllogism to be valid the unstated premiss would have to be:
'All those who are in favour of planning are Communists.' An alternative and truer unstated premiss would be: 'All Communists are in favour of planning,' but the syllogism would not then be valid.

4. (i) In a simplified form the argument could be represented thus:
'Some subtle opinions are not true;
Some fashionable opinions are subtle;
Therefore some unfashionable views are true.'
This is not valid. No conclusion can be drawn from the two premisses as the middle term is undistributed.
'Subtle opinions' and 'fashionable opinions' are necessarily vague terms and do not admit of clear-cut classifications. To attempt to apply a two-valued logic to them is an illogical thing to do.

(ii) 'All people who agree with me are right-minded; (unstated),
Some M.P.'s are people who agree with me;
therefore some M.P.'s are right-minded.'
Formally valid. No comment necessary.

(iii) This could only be expressed as a syllogism in a very artificial way.

The argument runs:

'Narrow-mindedness produces kill-joys;

The right sort of Education produces broad-mindedness;

therefore the teaching profession (? only) can make us joyful.'

It is assumed that the 'broad-mindedness' produced by Education is the contradictory of the 'narrow-mindedness' that kills joy: everyone might not agree with this. There is also the implication in the conclusion that *only* by being properly educated can we be happy, and this certainly cannot be derived from the premisses. Clearly there is something in the argument but it is overstated.

5. At least 39 and at most 59 are both.

6. (i), (iii), (v), (vi), (vii).   7. (i), (iii).

8. (iii), (iv).   9. (ii), (iii).   10. (ii), (iv), (v).

11.
$$\frac{M\,a\,P}{S\,a\,M} \quad \frac{M\,e\,P}{S\,a\,M} \quad \frac{M\,a\,P}{S\,i\,M} \quad \frac{M\,e\,P}{S\,i\,M}$$
$$S\,a\,P \qquad S\,e\,P \qquad S\,i\,P \qquad S\,o\,P$$

12.
$$\frac{P\,e\,M}{S\,a\,M} \quad \frac{P\,a\,M}{S\,e\,M} \quad \frac{P\,e\,M}{S\,i\,M} \quad \frac{P\,a\,M}{S\,o\,M}$$
$$S\,e\,P \qquad S\,e\,P \qquad S\,o\,P \qquad S\,o\,P$$

13.
$$\frac{M\,a\,P}{M\,a\,S} \quad \frac{M\,i\,P}{M\,a\,S} \quad \frac{M\,a\,P}{M\,i\,S} \quad \frac{M\,e\,P}{M\,a\,S} \quad \frac{M\,o\,P}{M\,a\,S} \quad \frac{M\,e\,P}{M\,i\,S}$$
$$S\,i\,P \qquad S\,i\,P \qquad S\,i\,P \qquad S\,o\,P \qquad S\,o\,P \qquad S\,o\,P$$

14.
$$\frac{P\,a\,M}{M\,a\,S} \quad \frac{P\,a\,M}{M\,e\,S} \quad \frac{P\,i\,M}{M\,a\,S} \quad \frac{P\,e\,M}{M\,a\,S} \quad \frac{P\,e\,M}{M\,i\,S}$$
$$S\,i\,P \qquad S\,e\,P \qquad S\,i\,P \qquad S\,o\,P \qquad S\,o\,P$$

CHAPTER 7

1. (i) Psychological certainty.

(ii) If the statement is correct it is one of *necessity* and not mere psychological certainty.

(iii) Mathematical probability based on equally likely events, also psychological expectation.

(iv) Psychological expectation.

(v) Psychological certainty; it may be very strongly supported by the evidence.

(vi) A confident forecast about the future.

(vii) As for (vi).

(viii) These are all statements of psychological uncertainty or certainty: for the first three 'probably's' it looks as though the sums have not yet been worked out, or all the evidence is not yet available. But the writer feels that he has got enough evidence to be *sure* that it will be quicker. In the last sentence the writer states it as his opinion that the organization will not be unscrambled.

2. (*a*) The chances are 100/5,000,000. The events are equally likely.

(*b*) The events are not equally likely. One is likely to meet more Middlesex number plates in Middlesex than in Yorkshire. The mathematical theory of probability does not apply. The figures may however help one to form a subjective estimate.

3. (i) True, because in general the events are equally likely.

(ii) Untrue. There are four equally likely possibilities: both heads; the first heads, the second tails; the first tails, the second heads; both tails. The probability of both heads is therefore 1/4.

(iii) Untrue. There are altogether 8 equally likely possibilities, as two heads and a tail can happen in 3 different ways and so can two tails and a head. The probability of three heads is therefore 1/8.

(iv) Untrue. Obviously.

(v) Untrue. It depends what the name is and how frequently it appears. The mathematical theory of probability does apply to this but more information is needed.

(vi) Untrue. The mathematical theory of probability does not apply. The fact that there are 10 Doctors, however, would help one to form a subjective estimate.

CHAPTER 8

1. (i) Efficient.

(ii) Probably efficient ('because it swerved, because I took my eye off it'), but the questioner might be implying that it was missed deliberately, in which case he would be in search of a final cause.

(iii) Either. 'Because it hasn't been cut' (efficient) might be regarded as a facetious answer, but 'because the gardener is ill' (also efficient, but taking the matter one stage further back) would probably be considered a satisfactory explanation. 'Because we want a crop of hay' (final) would also be a satisfactory answer.

(iv) Efficient (e.g. 'because I was held up in a traffic jam'). But the answer could be final—'because I didn't want to see the first act'.

(v) Very likely no answer is expected: it looks like a rebuke. The answer might be 'because I forgot to move it' (efficient) or 'Because I wanted to melt it to go with the asparagus' (final).

(vi) Efficient.

(vii) Efficient.

(viii) Probably final, the implication being 'Why does God allow so much suffering?' But the answer might give an efficient cause: 'Because man is so wicked.'

(ix) A silly question, almost unanswerable except by 'They just are'. One would have to question the questioner to find out exactly what it is that he wants to know.

(x) The questioner probably wants an analysis of wetness; a description rather than a cause. This is hardly a proper 'Why' question.

  2. x is caused by r, which is caused by D.

    y is caused by p, which is caused by C.

    z is caused by p, which is caused by C.

$$q \text{ is caused by } A \text{ or } E.$$

(Remember that a cause must always have the same effect, but an effect may have many different causes.

From (i), when A, B, C are present r is absent, $\therefore$ r is not caused by $A, B,$ or C.

From (ii), when B, D, E are present p is absent, $\therefore$ p is not caused by $B, D,$ or E, etc.)

  3. c can most simply be prevented by preventing B from happening.

(Consider first (v)-(ix). By arguments similar to those used in the last example it will be seen that c could not be caused by any single one of the events p, q, r, s, t, but could be caused by rt, prt, and various other combinations of 3 or more letters, all of which contain t. If t can be eliminated therefore c will be eliminated.

A similar study of (i)-(iv) will show that the possible combinations which can cause t all contain B. The elimination of B will therefore eliminate t and thus c.)

4. To prevent the widgets from wumbling refrain from taking off the lid; this will prevent the engine from boiling.

To prevent the stugs from sticking and the sprockets from falling off refrain from pressing button B; this will prevent the anemometer from quivering. (Method is as for questions 2 and 3.)

5. The explanation is, in the words of the letter: 'Rabbits used to keep the grass so short here that ragwort was unchecked by its natural enemy, grass; but with the onset of myxomatosis and consequent reduction of the rabbit population grass flourished and ragwort was suppressed.'

6. See Chapter X, p. 192.

CHAPTER 9

1. (i) An argument by analogy is implied. In fact scoring runs at cricket is not very similar to producing goods in industry; there are obvious reasons for the irregularity of the first which do not apply to the second. See (xi) of this same question.

(ii) For an accident to have been somebody's 'fault' a mistake, an error of judgement, must have been made. Anybody who was involved may in a sense have 'caused' the accident but this is not at all the same thing as to be to blame for it.

(iii) If everybody always waits for the other person to dip no dipping will ever take place.

(iv) A generalization is supported (? claimed to be proved) by a single, rather dubious example. Is 'giving a lecture on morality' a good example of 'personal merit'?

(v) 'Public interest' is used in two very different senses: (*a*) public advantage, (*b*) public curiosity.

(vi) This is an argument that could be (and often is) used against any improvement. The object of Ministries that did not exist before the war is to increase the welfare of the community, though there is obviously room for differences of opinion as to whether they succeed in doing this.

(vii) There is nothing illogical about an empirical (i.e. practical, derived from experience) approach to a very practical problem.

(viii) It is hard to see how the past can be modified.

(ix) Those who suggest that fox hunting is cruel would certainly say that the cruelty involved is to the fox. The fact that employment and pleasure are given to many people has no bearing on whether or no the sport is cruel, though it is a fact that might be put forward to justify or counterbalance the cruelty.

(x) It is certainly sensible to ask whether thin lips indicate certain characteristics, and it would be sensible to ask whether thin or thick nostrils do; but it cannot be sensible to ask whether a 'bewildered' look (i.e. the look which we have found from experience that people have when bewildered) indicates bewilderment, or sensitive nostrils sensitivity.

(xi) The analogy is not apt. Playing cricket is not like manufacturing goods. (See this same question, (i).)

(xii) The accusation of inconsistency rests on the assumption that Socialist intellectuals do in fact attribute the superiority of the proletariat entirely to the conditions which it is desired to abolish.

(xiii) The author claims that the phrase about 'man conquering nature' is confused because 'on any proper interpretation' nature includes man, and because a conquest can only be over other men. In fact when this phrase was used it is surely obvious that neither 'nature nor 'conquest' were used with these meanings.

2. (i) Not very apt. A bludgeon and a rapier are both used to wound or kill, not to examine or probe.

(ii) Somewhat mixed and not very accurate. Neither bolts nor boomerangs roost. The suggestion that the bolt came home to roost, like a boomerang, seems to imply that it came back to where it started, which was surely in the religious field rather than the economic. The point is thoroughly obscured.

3. (i) 'Men have agreed to banish from their society anyone who tolerates insults of various kinds without fighting a duel.

(ii) It is never unlawful to fight in self-defence.

(iii) He who fights a duel fights to prevent himself from being driven out of society—i.e. in self-defence.

(iv) ∴ a man may lawfully fight a duel.'

The 'self-defence' referred to in (ii) would usually mean defending oneself from physical assault; but in (iii) it is extended to mean defending oneself from an unpleasant happening. The argument might be extended even further to justify fighting to defend oneself from any unpleasant happening however trivial.

It might also be argued that there is a distinction between man-made laws, what 'men have agreed to . . .', and the laws of Christianity.

4. The implication is that 'relentless logic' treats classes as though the divisions were clear-cut and not 'cloudy at their edges'. Unfortunately this is an accusation that can sometimes fairly be brought against logicians and Wells's strictures are then justifiable. But in fact, as we have tried to show, to treat classes like this is not a logical but a highly illogical thing to do.

5. (i) Presumably the black limousine also has to bear a tax of 2s. 6d. on every gallon of fuel.

(ii) This argument begs the question. The implication is that just as man uses electricity to light London, so God uses gravitation to control the planets.

This is a fair comparison only for those who believe both these things to be true, which the writer of the letter clearly does and which Dr. Huxley clearly does not. The statement of the first is certainly not a proof or even a support of the second.

(iii) This would only be a justification if it were claimed that *only* discoveries were made possible by freedom, or if it were claimed that people could only keep their freedom if they employed it for *all* its possible uses.

(iv) The qualities required for a good 'peace-time pilot of the country' are not necessarily the same as those required for a good war-time pilot.

(v) 'In order to educate we must teach; in order to teach we must know. The things that we know must be true. The truth is everywhere the same.' So far, all right. But to infer that education should be everywhere the same is to make at least two assumptions which are certainly false: (1) that in educating people we teach them *all* the knowledge there is—in fact a great deal of selection must take place, (2) that education consists *only* of imparting knowledge.

6. (i) 'For the boxer, the doctor, the general, skill in defence implies also skill in attack. Therefore if one is good at preventing others from stealing, one will also be good at stealing.

But the just man is good at keeping money safe.

∴ the just man is a kind of thief.'

Two main mistakes. (1) Argument by analogy. (2) What makes a thief is the will to steal, a lack of respect for other people's rights, greed, starvation. The fact that one is good at keeping one's own property implies none of these things (though it might be true that such a person would be good at stealing if he wanted to).

(ii) 'The fact that an historian cannot see a pattern in history is no evidence that there is no pattern there, that we have shaken off the bondage of Laws of Nature.

'Indeed, the opposite; for bonds which we cannot see are harder to shake off than those we can.'

In other words:

Invisible bonds are hard to shake off,

X cannot see any bonds,

∴ they are hard to shake off,

∴ the presumption is that they are still there.

Comment is hardly necessary! The question is begged by the assumption that the bonds are there.

(iii) 'Eyes, ears have their functions which they can only perform with their characteristic virtues.

'Life is a function of mind and the mind will therefore have its peculiar virtue.

'Goodness enables the mind to perform its functions well.

'Justice is the peculiar virtue of the mind.

'∴ the just-minded man will have a good life and will be happy.

'∴ justice pays better than injustice.'

The core of this argument seems to be that because Goodness and Justice are both the characteristic virtue of the mind therefore the just-minded man will have a good life. It is very hard to see how this can be claimed to follow. There does not seem to be much connection between the 'goodness' which is the peculiar virtue of the mind and the 'good' (i.e. the prosperous) life. The main question appears to be begged and altogether this is a particularly nonsensical argument.

(iv) 'An over-inflated balloon bursts and the air is dispersed; so with an over-inflated economy and its money. The cause of economic inflation is obvious, but not so its effects: they may be that prices are raised or that prices are lowered. We decide which by a logical argument.

Suppose effect is that prices rise, then there is more money, but this is Inflation ∴ Inflation causes itself. But this is impossible ∴ effect is that prices fall.

'But what goes down must previously have gone up ∴ prices in the past must have risen, ∴ economy must have been producing more and is therefore now producing less because of Inflation.'

This argument is so obviously nonsensical that it is only necessary to comment very briefly.

A false analogy; 'Inflation' used in undefined and different senses; Inflation, like many other things, is cumulative and may, in a sense, cause itself: what goes down need not previously have gone up.

(v) 'If Baumann is correct about his suggested criteria for being one —namely being undivided and isolated—we should expect animals to have some idea of unity.

'But though a dog certainly distinguishes individual objects as isolated and undivided, it seems to me unlikely that it is conscious of the common element "one" in situations where it encounters one other dog or one cat.

'∴ the notion of unity becomes known to us through our higher intellectual powers.

'∴ properties which animals perceive as well as we do cannot be what is essential.'

Two questions are here being considered.

(1) What it is that is essential in our concept of unity—whether it is 'such properties of things as being undivided or being isolated' or whether it is something more than that.

(2) Whether a dog is 'capable of having some sort of idea of unity'.

It would clearly be possible, though not perhaps very rational, to assume that the concept can only be appreciated by man's higher intellectual powers and to infer that a dog is not capable of having this idea. It would also be possible, and rather more rational, to come to the conclusion from a study of the behaviour of dogs that they do not have an idea of what we mean by the word 'one' and to infer that this idea can therefore only be understood by man's higher intellectual powers.

The method which Frege has employed seems to be a question-begging mixture of the two.

While considering the question whether a dog has an idea of unity he assumes that the essence of the concept is not merely being un-divided and isolated, he therefore comes to the conclusion that it 'seems unlikely' that a dog has an idea of unity. He then infers that this idea can only be attained by man's higher intellectual powers and that therefore the essence of the concept is not merely being undivided and isolated.

The argument is seen to be completely circular.

(vi) 'However much the behaviour of the body seems to fit in with the theory of Materialism it is still sensible to ask the question: "Has it a mind?" But on the behaviouristic (or Materialistic) theory to have a mind means just to behave in certain ways, therefore, if the theory were true, to ask this question would be like asking whether a thing that behaves in certain ways behaves in certain ways. But the question *can* be raised, and therefore when we ascribe a mind to a body we do not simply mean that it behaves in certain ways.'

This argument clearly begs the question completely. It merely points out that the question 'Has it a mind?' will have a different mean-ing for those who believe in Materialism and for those who don't. All that one is entitled to say is: 'It is clear that when those of us who do not believe in Materialism ascribe a mind or a mental process to an external body we do not mean simply that it behaves in certain charac-teristic ways.'

7. The conclusion is clearly not true: beings (human) do terminate their existence by committing suicide. They can do so by taking action immediately before their existence is terminated (pistol, knife), or some time before (poison, gas-oven). The assumptions on which the pro-position is based are shown by experience to be false.

(It is possible of course that R. Jack might have argued that this is to misinterpret the meanings of any or all of the words 'being', 'ultimate cause', 'existence'. It would no doubt be possible to define them in such a way as to make the proposition analytic and therefore necessarily true.)

8. Professor Toynbee may use the word 'Europe' in this sense, but most people don't. It is more often used to denote a certain geographical area.

CHAPTER 10

1. Blue.

2. Some possible reasons: (i) Fewer matches; (ii) worse weather; (iii) less spare time; (iv) less attractive cricket; (v) more rival attractions; (vi) less interest in cricket because, e.g., more tennis played at school.

3. Going round the table in a clockwise direction: Harry Brown, the Politician; Mary Smith; Dick Green, the Dustman; Joan Brown; Tom Smith, the Architect; Nancy Green.

4. Brown is the heaviest, then Jones, then Smith.

5. (i) The number in each 5-year age group would always be less than that in the one before; the differences between successive age groups would be slight to start with and then increase. Consider effects of variations in birth-rates and death-rates, immigration, emigration, wars.

(ii) The effect is not great. The figures for 1955 were as follows:

Emigrants to U.S.A. and Commonwealth:	125,000
Immigrants from U.S.A. and Commonwealth:	80,000
Net loss of population	45,000

(iii) The worst of the bulge was between 5 and 14 in June 1957. Difficulties about secondary and University Education for the next 10 years.

6. In 1957 about 3,788,000 out of 51,657,000 were over 70. This is about 7·3 %. The birth-rate decreased steadily from 1900 to 1940. So did the death-rate. Methods of birth control were partly responsible for the former, improved medical skill and knowledge for the latter.

As a result, either the age of retirement has to be raised, or those who are in employment have to produce a greater surplus over what they need to consume themselves, or the standard of living must fall. The first two of these have happened, but not the third.

The trend is likely to continue.

7. A, B, and E are wearing black discs; C and D are wearing white.

8. John: all true. James: all false.

Nancy: true, false, true. Lucy: true, false, true.

Pamela: all true.

Pamela is the mother of Nancy and the aunt of John and Lucy, who are brother and sister. John is married to his cousin Nancy, and they have one son, James.

(If Nancy's first statement is false she has at least one brother or sister, therefore at least every alternate statement is true, therefore her second statement is true, therefore she has a son. But she also has a brother or sister, therefore all her statements are true. But this is contrary to our hypothesis that her first statement is false. Therefore her first statement is true, and as she has no brothers or sisters her second statement is false and her third true. She must have a child, but it's not John. Argue similarly for Lucy and the rest follows easily.)

9. The following are among the points that might be raised: Better roads needed as well as more roads. Should the number of vehicles be restricted? Can more and better roads be afforded? Is the reason for the decrease in accidents that cars are safer or that drivers are more skilful and careful? How can the number of accidents be decreased even further?

10. (i) Yes. He is a member of the Nashum Club.

(ii) Yes. He is not a member of the Nashum Club.

(iii) No. Can't tell.

11. Present on Monday: B, C, D, E, F; Present on Tuesday: A, C, D, F, G; Present on Wednesday: A, B, C, D, G; Present on Thursday: C, E, F; Present on Friday: B, C, E, F.

Charlie is the Bottle-Washer.

(D (2) is a starting-point. If true, D never tells truth $\therefore$ false, $\therefore$ D could not have been there for more than $2\frac{1}{2}$ days, $\therefore$ D was there for $2\frac{1}{2}$ days exactly, $\therefore$ there on Wednesday, and D (1) true. $\therefore$ F there for 4 days, $\therefore$ F (1) and (2) both true, $\therefore$ E (1) and (2) both true ... etc.)

12. Alf: Bottle-Washer £18 18s. od.
    Bert: Door-Shutter, £15 15s. od.
    Charlie: Door-Knob Polisher, £15 5s. od.
    Duggie: Worker, £15 10s. od.
    Ernie: Welfare Officer: £15 os. od.
    Fred: Sweeper-Upper, £15 15s. od.
    George: Door-Opener, £12 8s. od.

(Names and occupations are abbreviated to their initials. It will be found helpful to set down in a table with rows marked A, B, C, etc. and columns marked D-K-P, S-U, etc. all information about occupations as it becomes available by putting ticks or crosses in the appropriate squares. Consider G (1). If false G is W, but W always tells truth, ∴ G (1) cannot be false. ∴ G not W. If G (2) true, B's statements both false, ∴ B is D-O, ∴ one of B's statements true and one false. ∴ G (2) not true. ∴ G's statements alternately true and false, ∴ G either D-O or D-S. ∴ C (1) false, ∴ F (1) false, ∴ B (1) false, ∴ neither B, C, nor F can be W-O, W or B-W. If B (2) false then B is D-O, but B (1) also false ∴ B cannot be D-O, ∴ B (2) true. ∴ B is D-S. ∴ G is D-O. ∴ if anyone else makes a false remark all his remarks are false. ∴ C (2) and F (2) are both false. ∴ C and F are D-K-P and S-U, not necessarily respectively; and A, D, E are W-O, W and B-W, not necessarily respectively. ∴ all remarks made by A; D and E are true. From D (1), D not WO. From G (3) F not D-K-P, ∴ F is S-U and C is D-K-P. Consider wages. From A (1), A : B = 6 : 5, from A (2), B : E = 21 : 20; from E (1), A's new wage is 27/25 ($\frac{108}{100}$) of A's old wage; ∴ A's wage is a multiple of 27. Since A's wage is also a multiple of 6 and 21 and is less than 400s. it must be 378s. B's wage is therefore 315s and E's 300s. The rest follows fairly simply.)

13. Alf is the Door-Shutter, is married to Ethel and makes remarks (3), (12), (18).

Bert is the Door-Knob Polisher, is married to Clarissa, and makes remarks (6), (8), (19).

Charlie is the Bottle-Washer, is married to Flossie, and makes remarks (4), (13), (16).

Duggie is the Worker, is married to Beatrice, and makes remarks (5), (7), (20).

Q

Ernie is the Welfare Officer, is married to Gertie, and makes remarks (1), (11), (21).

Fred is the Door-Opener, is married to Agnes, and makes remarks (2), (15), (17).

George is the Sweeper-Upper, is married to Diana and makes remarks (9), (10), (14).

(Important, as in the last example, to set out all information in tabular form as it becomes available. $1 + 2 + 3 \ldots + 21 = 231$. $231 \div 7 = 33$. $\therefore$ each man's total is 33 except for Duggie and Fred, one of whom must have a total of 32 and the other 34. Consider (13), (16), (20): at least 2 of these must be false, $\therefore$ at least 2 must be by Charlie; these 2 must be (13) and (16) as otherwise total greater than 33. $\therefore$ Charlie's 3rd remark must be (4), which is true. (20) is not by Charlie and is therefore true. (9) is not by Charlie and is therefore true. (3) is true, because no man's name comes into it. $\therefore$ (17) and (18) are both true or both false. If both false, both made by Ernie, which is impossible $(17 + 18 = 35)$, $\therefore$ both true. $\therefore$ (1) is false, $\therefore$ (1) is by Ernie. (12) is false, $\therefore$ (12) is by Alf. E's other two remarks must be (21), (11) or (20), (12) or (19), (13) or (18), (14) or (17), (15); but (12), (13), (17), (18) are all known not to be by Ernie. $\therefore$ (21), (11) are by Ernie … etc.)

14. A lives at No. 8, B at No. 36, C at No. 49.

(Each person thinks that the numbers of the other two are either above or not above 23 (> 23 or $\not> 23$), a perfect square or not a perfect square (sq or $\overline{\text{sq}}$), a multiple of 4 or not a multiple of 4 (m (4) or $\overline{\text{m}}$ (4)).)

The combinations of these alternatives with the possibilities in each case are:

  (i) > 23, sq, m (4): 36, 64.
 (ii) > 23, sq, $\overline{\text{m}}$ (4): 25, 49.
(iii) > 23, $\overline{\text{sq}}$, m (4): 24, 28, 32, 40, 44, etc.
 (iv) > 23, $\overline{\text{sq}}$, $\overline{\text{m}}$ (4): 26, 27, 29, 30, etc.
  (v) $\not> 23$, sq, m (4): 4, 16.
 (vi) $\not> 23$, sq, $\overline{\text{m}}$ (4): 1, 9.
(vii) $\not> 23$, $\overline{\text{sq}}$, m (4): 8, 12, 20.
(viii) $\not> 23$, $\overline{\text{sq}}$, $\overline{\text{m}}$ (4): 2, 3, 5, 6, 7, etc.

A and C both think they know the number of B's house, but as A thinks that B always tells the truth and C thinks that B always lies, the information which they think they have about B's number is directly contradictory. Pairs of contradictories are (i) and (viii), (ii) and (vii), (iii) and (vi), (iv) and (v).

If A, B, or C thought that the number of one of the other two was in a group containing only one number they could announce it, but there is no group containing only one number. They will only be able to announce it when they think it is in a group containing two numbers if the number of their own house is in the group. A announces two numbers, those of B and C, but he does not know which is which. He must therefore either think that B and C are both in the same group in which there are two possibilities, or he must think that B and C are in the same group in which there are three numbers of which his own house is one. It is not possible for any of them to think that any of those whose numbers they announce is in a group containing more than three numbers. (ii) and (vii) is the only contradictory pair of which one group does not contain more than three numbers.

∴ A's number must be one of group (vii): 8, 12 or 20, and he must think that B and C are the other two. C's number must be one of group (ii): 25 or 49, and he must think that B is the other one.

The rest follows fairly simply.

Index